BEADS USED FOR THE PROJECTS IN

Beads are available in an astoundingly wide range of colors, shape
Below are brief descriptions of the beads used for the projects in this book.
Please feel free to make substitutions, if you like.

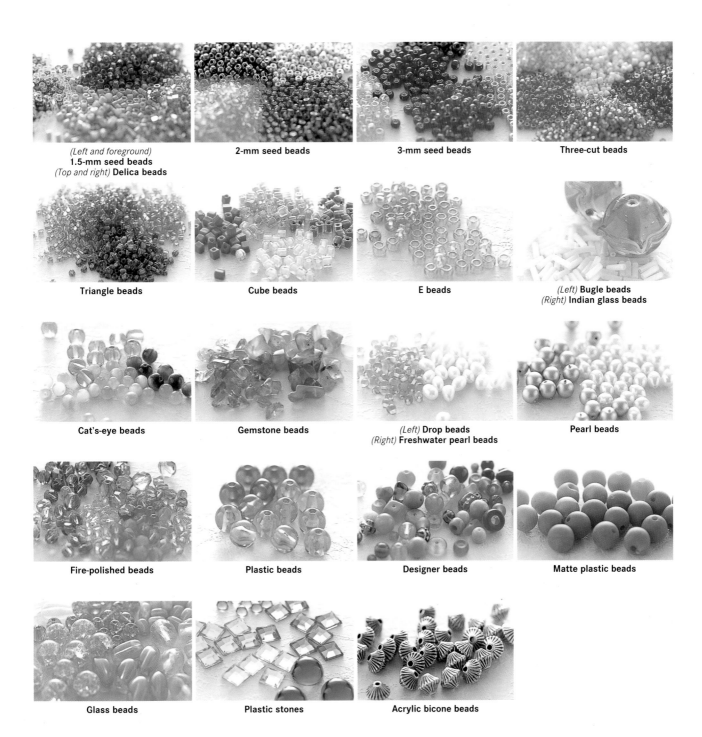

(Left and foreground)
1.5-mm seed beads
(Top and right) **Delica beads**

2-mm seed beads

3-mm seed beads

Three-cut beads

Triangle beads

Cube beads

E beads

(Left) **Bugle beads**
(Right) **Indian glass beads**

Cat's-eye beads

Gemstone beads

(Left) **Drop beads**
(Right) **Freshwater pearl beads**

Pearl beads

Fire-polished beads

Plastic beads

Designer beads

Matte plastic beads

Glass beads

Plastic stones

Acrylic bicone beads

1

Freehand

Contents

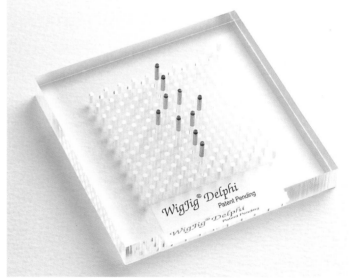

WigJig Delphi

Twist 'n' Curl

Wire Worker

Freehand

FREEHAND PROJECTS

Since wire is so flexible, you can shape it any way you like. Don't hesitate to make substitutions.
Let your imagination be your guide.

Necklace, Bracelet & Ring

These three pieces were inspired by flower garlands.
The leaves made of beads strung on wire add an airy quality, and the pale colors a touch of elegance.

Instructions: p. 34

4

Necklaces
These easy-to-make,
fanciful necklaces combine four types of beads
and four colors of wire.
Instructions: p. 33

5

5

Necklace & Bracelet

7

6

Necklace ◆ Bracelet

The irregular curves of the wire enhance
the beauty of these striking pieces.
Instructions: p. 36

Necklace & Bracelet

9

Necklace ◆ Bracelet
The gentle curves of the wire and the subtle colors
of the beads give these pieces a royal look.
Instructions: p. 37

8

Rings

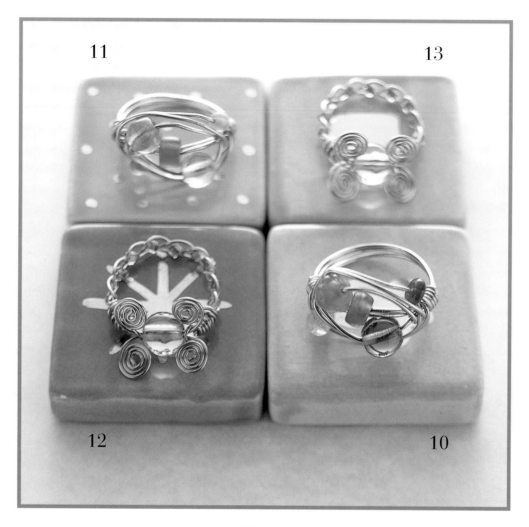

Rings

These rings were designed to emphasize the beauty
of both the beads and the wire.

Instructions: p. 38

14

15

16

Brooches

Brooches

These brooches exude warmth that only handmade
jewelry can. They look wonderful on hats,
handbags, and lapels.

Instructions: p. 40

WigJig Delphi

Jewelry made using the WigJig Delphi

The delicate, beautiful curves of wire are the main attraction of these pieces.
When you use a pegboard like WigJig Delphi, you can make any number of identical components.
And you don't have to worry about mistakes – you won't make any!

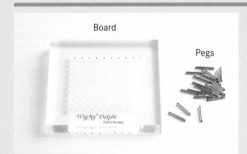
Board
Pegs

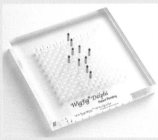
Nylon spacers
Super pegs

WigJig Delphi Set

To use this tool, you insert pegs into the board and wrap wire around them.

Super peg and spacer set

Super pegs and spacers expand your design possibilities. They are inserted into the pegboard, like the regular pegs

Further information about using this tool can be found in the instructions for Project #17 (shown on p. 11) on p. 50.

1 Grasp end of wire with round-nosed pliers.

2 Round end of wire.

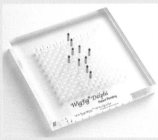

3 Arrange pegs on pegboard as indicated.

Starting point

4 Place rounded end of wire on peg at starting point.

5 Shape wire by wrapping it around the pegs.

6 Once your design is completed, remove wire from pegboard. Flatten wire with chain-nose pliers, and cut excess. Place a cloth between wire and pliers to avoid marring the wire.

Necklace, Bracelet and Ring

These pieces, worked in silver wire and capri blue beads, feature an innovative technique
that encloses beads in wire coils.

Instructions: p. 50

19

17

18

Necklace, Bracelet & Ring

11

22

20

21

Necklace, Bracelet and Earring

These light, airy pieces combine wire and beaded wire motifs.
Instructions: p. 52

Chain Belt

This belt is adorned with butterfly motifs. Adjust the length to your liking.

Instructions: p. 49

Chain Belt

23

Necklace
This simple but striking design
features beads enclosed in wire circles.
Instructions: p. 56

24

25

Necklace

Twist 'n' Curl

Jewelry made using Twist 'n' Curl

With Twist 'n' Curl, you can make beautiful, sturdy coils from fine-gauge wire in minutes.
You can add volume to a piece by coiling wire on which beads have been strung.

Twist 'n' Curl Set

This is a tool used to wind wire into coils (spirals). It comes in several sizes.

■HOW TO MAKE A BEADED WIRE BEAD

Beaded wire bead

Further information about using Twist 'n' Curl can be found in the instructions for #26 (shown on p. 16) on p. 57.

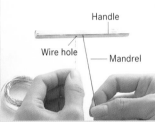

Handle

Wire hole — Mandrel

1 Using the thinner mandrel, insert fine-gauge wire on which beads have been strung into the wire hole. Rotate handle two or three times to secure the wire.

2 Holding the mandrel in one hand, wind the wire around it (about 2cm) by rotating the handle with your other hand.

3 Wind the section of wire on which beads have been strung in the same way. Wind it tightly enough so that there are no spaces between the beads.

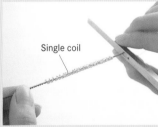

Single coil

4 After you have wound the section with beads on it, wind about 2cm more wire. Cut wire and remove coil from the mandrel.

5 Cut the 2-cm wire ends of the single coil in half. Insert a length of heavier wire into the single coil.

6 Using the thicker mandrel, insert the heavier wire into the wire hole. Wind the wire for 2cm, and then wind the single coil.

7 After you have wound the single coil, wind 2cm more wire. Cut wire and remove from mandrel. You have completed a beaded wire bead.

■HOW TO MAKE A WIRE BEAD (refer to instructions for making a beaded wire bead)

1 Using the thinner mandrel, make a single coil using only fine-gauge wire. Insert heavier wire into the single coil. Wind the heavier wire around the thicker mandrel.

2 Remove coil from bar and shape so that the center is wider than the ends.

Necklace

Necklace

The spherical sections of this necklace
were inspired by summer berries

Instructions: p. 57

27

16

26

Choker

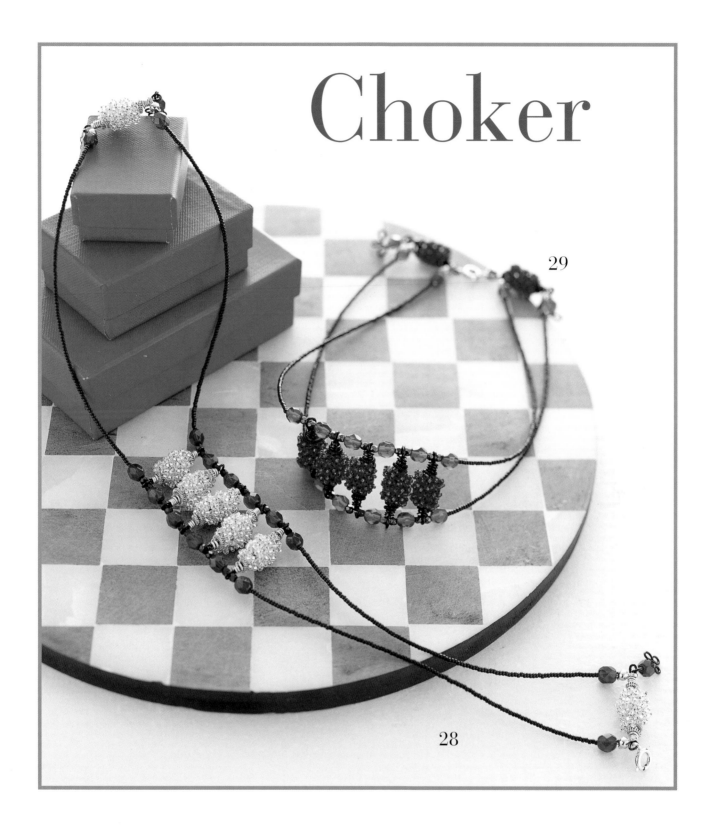

29

28

Choker
This eye-catching choker has beaded wire beads at its center.
The handmade clasp lends extra elegance.
Instructions: p. 58

31

Necklace ◆ Earrings

The natural colors used in these pieces and the intricate components add up to a look that is both [subtle and dramatic].

Instructions: p. 59

30

32

Choker

Choker

When you wear this lovely choker,
you'll look as though you emerged from a fairy tale.
Instructions: p. 60

Cell Phone Straps

35

34

33

Cell phone straps
Make a fashion statement with your cell phone
by creating one of these straps.
Instructions: p. 61

Necklace

Necklace

The colored wire components
give this necklace
an exquisite balance.
You're sure to be noticed!
Instructions: p. 62

36

Wire Worker

Jewelry made using the Wire Worker

The Wire Worker makes it easy to form heavier wire into a variety of shapes.
The cylinders it produces are large enough to encircle beads.

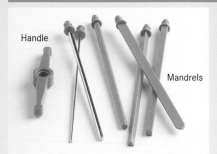

Handle

Mandrels

Wire Worker set

This tool helps you wind wire into coils (spirals) of different shapes. It comes with round (three sizes), flat, square, and triangular mandrels.

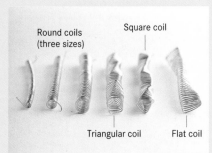

Round coils (three sizes)

Square coil

Triangular coil

Flat coil

The ends of the bars are screws that attach to the center of the handle. You can make many types of coils with the six mandrels.

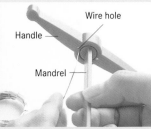

Wire hole

Handle

Mandrel

1 This tool works is used in the same way as Twist 'n' Curl (see p. 15).
Insert the wire into the wire hole and wrap it around the handle two or three times to secure.

2 Hold the mandrel in one hand, and rotate the handle with the other, winding the wire around the mandrel.
Note: If you're using plastic mandrels, avoid winding the wire too tightly. You may have trouble removing it.

Coiling Gizmo

This tool isn't used to make any of the projects in this book, but like Twist 'n' Curl and Wire Worker, it is used to form wire coils. Since it comes with a bracket, you can fasten it to a board or other surface and make beautiful coils quickly and easily.

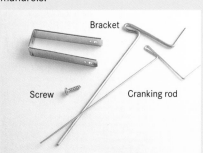

Bracket

Screw

Cranking rod

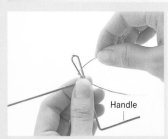

Handle

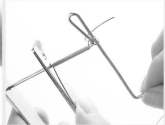

1 Wind wire around cranking rod two or three times.

2 Insert bar into hole in bracket. Hold wire parallel to side of bracket, Rotate handle, winding wire around cranking rod.

3 Cut wire and remove coil from cranking rod.
Note: You can use Coiling Gizmo without the bracket. See instructions for Twist 'n' Curl on p. 15.

Bracelet & Earrings

Bracelet ◆ Earrings

These primitive look of these striking pieces can be found only in handmade jewelry.

Instructions: p. 63

37

38

39

Necklaces & Bracelets

Necklaces and Bracelets

These elegant pieces are reminiscent of ethnic jewelry.

Instructions: p. 64

Decorative Items for the Home

These designs will transform ordinary household articles into works of art.

Decorated Photo Frame

44

Decorated Photo Frame

When light shines on this transparent frame, the wire and beads sparkle beautifully. Adjust the arrangement to suit your frame.

Instructions: p. 54

Decorations
for Glass Candle Holders

45

46

Decorations for Glass Candle Holders
Transform drinking glasses into lovely candle holders.
These make wonderful gifts.
Instructions: p. 39

Jewelry or Card Stands

Jewelry or Card Stands
You can hang your earrings or cards, or anything you like, on these stands. We're sure you will find many uses for them.
Instructions: p. 43

47

48

Mini-Rack

49

Mini-Rack

This mini-rack, with its leaf motif, has a door that opens.
You can use it to hold flowers,
but it is quite impressive on its own.
Instructions: p. 44

50

Glass Decoration
We used the same leaf motif to decorate this glass.
Fill it with flowers or candy, or whatever strikes your fancy.
Instructions: p. 46

Decorations
for Glass Candle Holders

52

51

53

Decorations for Glass Candle Holders
We have adorned these glass candle holders with
wire spirals and small beads. Adjust the shape of the
decorations to fit your glass.
Instructions: p. 48

Bottle Decorations

54

55

Bottle Decorations
These designs feature silver wire and plastic stones in cool colors, and are perfect for bottles with simple lines, or bud vases.
Instructions: p. 42

TOOLS AND SUPPLIES

Pliers and cutters

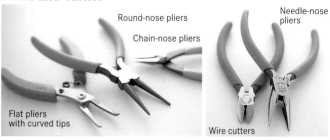

Round-nose pliers

Chain-nose pliers

Needle-nose pliers

Flat pliers with curved tips

Wire cutters

Needle-nose pliers: Serrated jaws ensure a firm grip; these can also be used to cut wire.
Wire cutters
Round-nose pliers: Used to bend and curve wire
Flat pliers with curved tips: Their narrow tips make these pliers perfect for working with findings.
Chain-nose pliers: Their smooth jaws allow you to work with wire without marring it.

Jewelry findings

Clasp set *(left)*: Convenient because it includes jump rings
Ear wires *(right)*: Use earring backs if you don't have pierced ears.

Crimp beads *(left)*: Used to finish and secure the ends of a piece; about 2mm in diameter
Jump rings *(center)*: These measure 3 x 4mm, and are used to join sections of a piece
Bead tips *(right)*: Termination devices for bead strands

Stickpin *(top)*: Comes with a safety catch.
Perforated pin back *(bottom)*

Perforated brooch back *(left)*
Perforated pendant back *(right)*

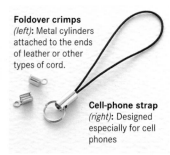

Eyepins *(left)*: These are inserted into beads and joined to other sections of a piece.
Spring clasp *(right)*: Fasteners attached to the ends of necklaces and bracelets

Foldover crimps *(left)*: Metal cylinders attached to the ends of leather or other types of cord.

Cell-phone strap *(right)*: Designed especially for cell phones

Adjustable chain closure *(left)*: Allows you to adjust the length of a necklace when attached to a clasp.
Clasp set with adjustable chain closure *(right)*: Also includes jump rings.

Copper Wire

Its flexibility and hardness make copper wire the best choice for jewelry-making. It comes in several gauges; the higher the number, the finer the gauge.

28-gauge copper wire: 0.35mm diameter

22-gauge copper wire: 0.7mm diameter

20-gauge copper wire: 0.9mm diameter

18-gauge copper wire: 1.2mm diameter

Leather cord
Genuine leather; comes in several sizes

Nylon-coated wire
Strong, smooth, fine wire coated with nylon

Nylon thread
Comes in several sizes (the smaller the number, the finer the thread) and colors.

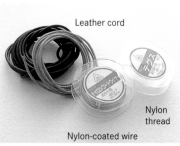

Leather cord

Nylon thread

Nylon-coated wire

Glue
Fast-drying two-part epoxy *(right)*: Suitable for metal findings, beads, leather, etc.
Industrial strength multi-purpose adhesive *(left)*: Suitable for hard plastics, glass, ceramic, and wood. Do not use superglue, because it discolors some beads.

Fimo Soft polymer clay
Fimo Soft hardens when baked in a kitchen oven. It comes in many colors and finishes, including pearlescent, translucent and fluorescent.

No. 4, 5 (p. 5)
Supplies

No. 4 (Necklace)
Copper wire: 28-gauge wire (1m each brown, dark blue, aqua and purple)
Beads: 13 5-mm yellow-green "E" beads, 2.5-mm triangle beads (39 pale blue, 75 pink), 84 2-mm silver seed beads, amethyst beads measuring 7cm when lined up (about 13), new jade beads measuring 5cm when lined up (about 9)
Findings: 7-mm bronze spring clasp, bronze adjustable chain closure

No. 5 (Necklace)
Copper wire: 28-gauge wire (1m each brown, magenta, green and purple)
Beads: 13 5-mm pale blue "E" beads, 2.5-mm triangle beads (39 light blue, 75 green), 84 2-mm round bronze seed beads, red agate beads measuring 7cm when lined up (about 13), new jade beads measuring 5cm when lined up (about 9)
Findings: 7-mm bronze spring clasp, bronze adjustable chain closure

✳ *No. 4 and No. 5 differ in colors used only.*

Instructions for No. 4, 5

1. String beads on the four 1-m lengths wire (string "E" beads and gemstone beads singly, and seed beads and triangle beads 3 at a time).

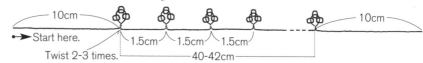

Start here.
Twist 2-3 times.
10cm
1.5cm 1.5cm 1.5cm
40-42cm
10cm

Arrangement of beads: Colors in parentheses are for No. 5

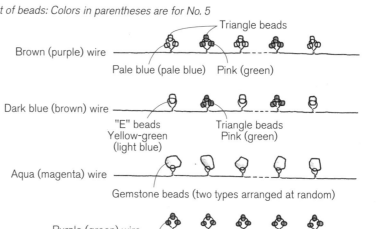

Triangle beads
Brown (purple) wire
Pale blue (pale blue)   Pink (green)

Dark blue (brown) wire
"E" beads
Yellow-green (light blue)
Triangle beads
Pink (green)

Aqua (magenta) wire
Gemstone beads (two types arranged at random)

Purple (green) wire
Seed beads: Silver (bronze)

2. Align four strands wire at one side and twist. Weave wire loosely as if you were making a four-strand braid.

3. Gather wires at other end of necklace together and twist, as you did at the beginning. Attach findings.

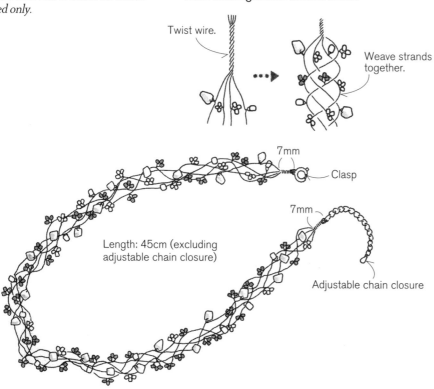

Twist wire.
Weave strands together.

7mm
Clasp
7mm
Adjustable chain closure
Length: 45cm (excluding adjustable chain closure)

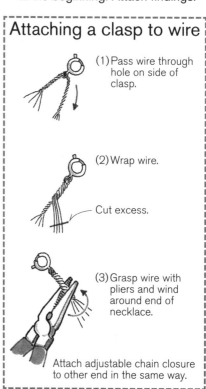

Attaching a clasp to wire

(1) Pass wire through hole on side of clasp.

(2) Wrap wire.
Cut excess.

(3) Grasp wire with pliers and wind around end of necklace.

Attach adjustable chain closure to other end in the same way.

33

No. 1, 2, 3 (p. 4)
Supplies

No. 1 (Necklace)

Copper wire: 350cm 28-gauge white wire

Beads: 20 4.5-5-mm white freshwater pearl beads, 2-2.5-mm three-cut beads (78 pink, 384 pale green), 15 3.4-mm blue drop beads, 140 2-mm beige seed beads, 5-mm round designer beads (1 pink, 6 beige)

Other supplies: 15-mm gold perforated pendant back, 7-mm gold spring clasp, gold adjustable chain closure, 60cm No. 2 clear nylon thread

No. 2 (Bracelet)

Copper wire: 2m 28-gauge white wire

Beads: 15 white 4.5-5-mm freshwater pearl beads, 2-2.5-mm three-cut beads (52 pink, 208 pale green), 11 3.4-mm blue drop beads, 95 2-mm beige seed beads, 5 x 10-mm oval designer beads with squared ends (1 pink, 4 beige)

Other supplies: 15-mm perforated round gold clasp, 60cm No. 2 clear nylon thread

No. 3 (Ring)

Copper wire: 120cm 28-gauge white wire

Beads: 2 white 4.5-5-mm freshwater pearl beads, 2-2.5-mm three-cut beads (20 pink, 28 pale green), 2 3.4-mm blue drop beads, 18 2-mm beige seed beads, 5-mm round pink designer bead

Instructions for No. 1

1. Make flower for center of necklace.

60cm nylon thread

Seed bead

Freshwater pearl bead

Follow the arrows as you work.

Pendant back

Designer bead (pink)

Continue from here.

Leave a 5-cm end.

Starting point

Three-cut beads (pale green)

Drop bead

Continue from here.

Tie to 5-cm end at beginning of work, pass through pendant back and beads 2-3 times, and cut excess.

(1) Pass 150cm wire through pendant back; fold in half.

(2) Twist wires together (5mm).

(3) Attach base of pendant back.
(Bend tabs on back inward to secure.)

3. Attach findings.

Clasp

Adjustable chain closure

5-6mm

Pass wire through hole in clasp; twist 5-6mm (see p. 33).

2. Twist wire as you pass it through beads. (Unless otherwise indicated, spaces should be 6mm long. Work left and right sides in mirror image.)

Length: 35cm (excluding adjustable chain closure)

Twist 2-3 times.

Designer bead (beige)

Three-cut beads (pink)

Drop bead

Three-cut beads (pink)

Three-cut beads (pale green)

Start here.

Freshwater pearl bead

Seed beads

4. Attach necklace to flower.

Attach necklace to pendant back. (Follow procedure described in 3.)

Starting point
Center of 50cm wire

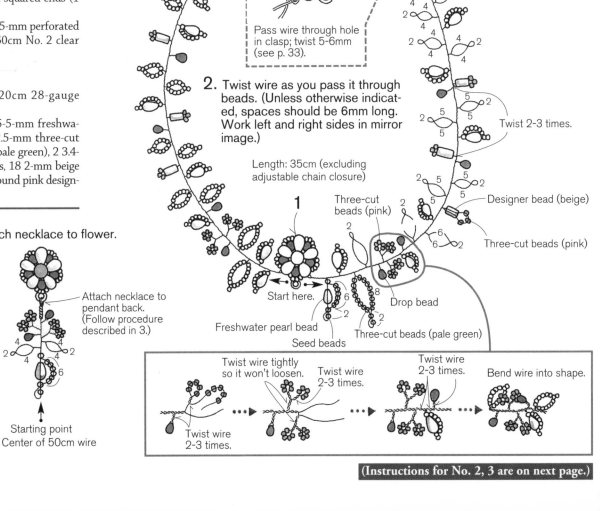

Twist wire 2-3 times.

Twist wire tightly so it won't loosen.

Twist wire 2-3 times.

Twist wire 2-3 times.

Bend wire into shape.

(Instructions for No. 2, 3 are on next page.)

Instructions for No. 2

1. Make flower.

60cm nylon thread

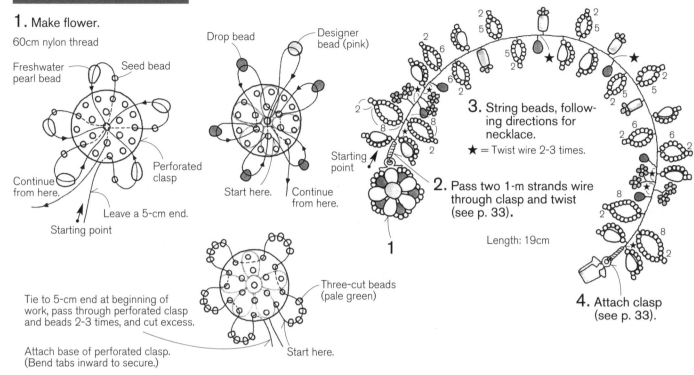

Freshwater pearl bead
Seed bead

Drop bead
Designer bead (pink)

Continue from here.

Leave a 5-cm end.

Starting point

Perforated clasp

Start here.
Continue from here.

Starting point

Tie to 5-cm end at beginning of work, pass through perforated clasp and beads 2-3 times, and cut excess.

Attach base of perforated clasp. (Bend tabs inward to secure.)

Start here.

Three-cut beads (pale green)

3. String beads, following directions for necklace.

★ = Twist wire 2-3 times.

2. Pass two 1-m strands wire through clasp and twist (see p. 33).

Length: 19cm

4. Attach clasp (see p. 33).

Instructions for No. 3

1. Make band.

60cm wire

Form a four-strand circle of desired diameter from wire. Tie to secure.

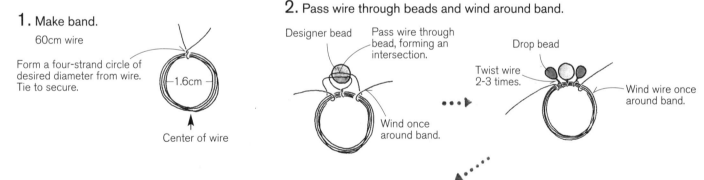

1.6cm

Center of wire

2. Pass wire through beads and wind around band.

Designer bead
Pass wire through bead, forming an intersection.

Drop bead

Twist wire 2-3 times.

Wind once around band.

Wind wire once around band.

3. Wind wire around band.

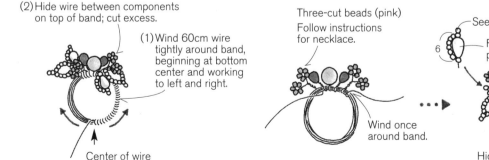

(2) Hide wire between components on top of band; cut excess.

(1) Wind 60cm wire tightly around band, beginning at bottom center and working to left and right.

Center of wire

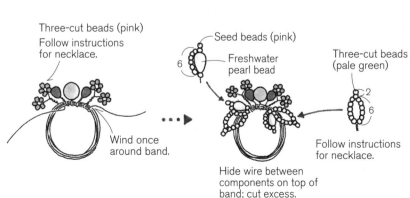

Three-cut beads (pink)
Follow instructions for necklace.

Wind once around band.

Seed beads (pink)
Freshwater pearl bead

6

Three-cut beads (pale green)

2
6

Follow instructions for necklace.

Hide wire between components on top of band; cut excess.

No. 6, 7 (p. 6)

Supplies

No. 6 (Necklace)
Copper wire: 1m 18-gauge silver wire
Beads: 10g (about 20) assorted green designer beads
Other supplies: 90cm 2-mm natural leather cord, 4 2-mm silver foldover crimps, 4 3 x 4-mm silver jump rings, 7-mm silver spring clasp, silver adjustable chain closure

No. 7 (Bracelet)
Copper wire: 360cm 18-gauge silver wire
Beads: 30g (about 46) assorted green designer beads

Instructions for No. 7

1. Make 3 sections of bracelet.

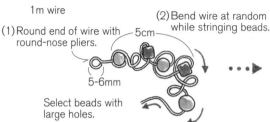

1m wire

(1) Round end of wire with round-nose pliers.

(2) Bend wire at random while stringing beads.

5cm

5-6mm

Select beads with large holes.

Shape wire and beads into a square.

4cm

Form circles on both sides of middle section only.

2. Join the 3 sections and attach hooks to each end, as shown below.

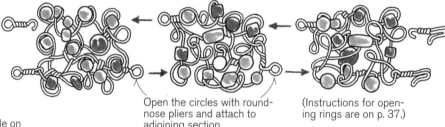

Open the circles with round-nose pliers and attach to adjoining section.

(Instructions for opening rings are on p. 37.)

How to make a hook

(1) Bend a 12-cm length wire.
8cm
4cm

(2) Bend end with round-nose pliers.
1cm

(3) Form a circle.
1cm
Round with pliers.

(4) Wind longer strand around base of circle.
Cut wire.
5mm
2cm

Make the eye.
5-6mm
2cm

Instructions for No. 6

1. Make pendant framework.

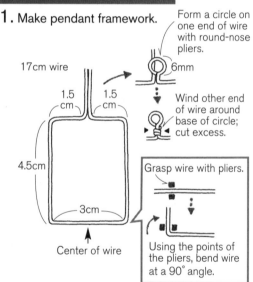

17cm wire

1.5 cm   1.5 cm

4.5cm

3cm

Center of wire

Form a circle on one end of wire with round-nose pliers.
6mm
Wind other end of wire around base of circle; cut excess.

Grasp wire with pliers.

Using the points of the pliers, bend wire at a 90° angle.

2. Fill framework with wire and beads.

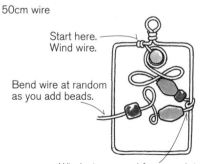

50cm wire

Start here. Wind wire.

Bend wire at random as you add beads.

Wind wire around framework in several locations to secure.

3. Attach leather cord.

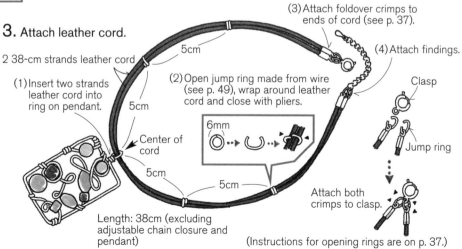

2 38-cm strands leather cord

(1) Insert two strands leather cord into ring on pendant.

5cm

5cm

Center of cord

5cm

5cm

5cm

(2) Open jump ring made from wire (see p. 49), wrap around leather cord and close with pliers.
6mm

(3) Attach foldover crimps to ends of cord (see p. 37).

(4) Attach findings.
Clasp
Jump ring
Attach both crimps to clasp.

Length: 38cm (excluding adjustable chain closure and pendant)

(Instructions for opening rings are on p. 37.)

No. 8, 9 (p. 7)
Supplies

No. 8 (Necklace)
Copper wire: 35cm 20-gauge copper wire, 40cm 18-gauge copper wire
Beads: 1.5-mm seed beads (8 yellow, 12 purple), 4 6-mm round amethyst glass beads, 9 x 13-mm oval amethyst glass bead, 5-mm amethyst cat's-eye bead
Other supplies: 40cm 1.5-mm dark brown leather cord, 2 gold foldover crimps, 2 3 x 4-mm gold jump rings, 7-mm gold spring clasp, gold adjustable chain closure

No. 9 (Bracelet)
Copper wire: 2m copper 22-gauge wire
Beads: 30 4-mm white pearl beads, round gold-enameled pearl beads (20 each 3-mm and 4-mm beads), garnet beads measuring 8cm when lined up (about 30)

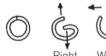

Instructions for No. 9

1. String beads on wire.

2m wire

Leave a 0.5-1cm space between beads.

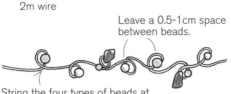

String the four types of beads at random; twist wire to secure.

2. Close the circle by winding ends of wire around piece, as shown below. Cut excess wire.

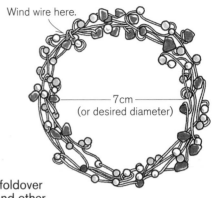

Wind wire here.

7cm (or desired diameter)

Instructions for No. 8

Adjustable chain closure

Clasp

40cm leather cord

Jump ring

4. Attach foldover crimp and other findings.

3. Wind wire around cords while stringing beads.

20cm 18-gauge wire

Start here; round end of wire.

6mm

3cm

Work opposite side in same way.

End here.

3 yellow seed beads
4 purple seed beads

Center of cord

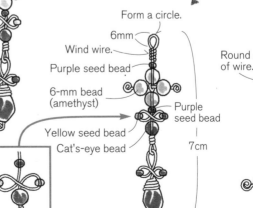

2. Pass cord through ring on pendant.

Form a circle.

6mm

Wind wire.

Purple seed bead

6-mm bead (amethyst)

Yellow seed bead

Cat's-eye bead

Purple seed bead

7cm

1. Make pendant.

15cm 20-gauge wire

9 x 13-mm amethyst bead

Form circle with pliers.

Start here.

Wind wire around beads.

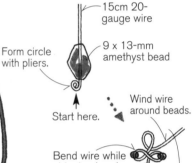

Bend wire while stringing beads (purple).

3cm

15cm 20-gauge wire

Start here. →

2cm

3.5cm 20-gauge wire

Round end of wire.

Leave a 4-mm space.

6-mm bead (amethyst)

Wrap wire once to secure.

No. 10, 11, 12, 13
(p. 8)
Supplies

No. 10 (Ring)

Copper wire: 70cm 20-gauge silver wire

Beads: 5 assorted purple designer beads (about 3g)

No. 11 (Ring)

Copper wire: 70cm 20-gauge silver wire

Beads: 5 assorted blue designer beads (about 3g)

No. 12 (Ring)

Copper wire: 110cm 22-gauge natural wire

Beads: 9 2.5-mm green triangle beads, 8-mm round yellow-green plastic bead

No. 13 (Ring)

Copper wire: 110cm 22-gauge silver wire

Beads: 9 2.5-mm blue triangle beads, 8-mm round pale blue plastic bead

---

* *No. 10, 11 and No. 12, 13 differ in colors used only.*

Instructions for No. 10, 11

1. Make a pattern with a diameter equivalent to desired finished size by wrapping a piece of paper around a pen or similar object.

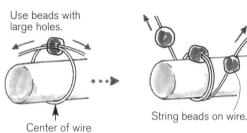

2. Wrap wire around pattern and string a bead on it, forming an intersection.

Use beads with large holes.

Center of wire

String beads on wire.

3. Wind wire around band while stringing beads.

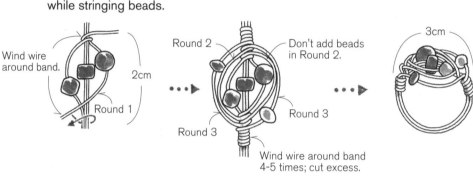

Wind wire around band.

Round 1

2cm

Round 2

Don't add beads in Round 2.

Round 3

Round 3

Wind wire around band 4-5 times; cut excess.

3cm

2. Form a circle at each end of band.

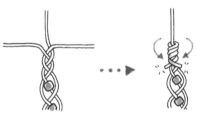

Bend wires at left and right. Wind them around wire at center. Cut excess.

3mm

Form a ring from wire at center. Wind end around other two wires; cut excess.

Instructions for No. 12, 13

1. Braid 3 strands wire while stringing beads.

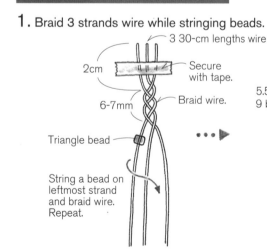

3 30-cm lengths wire

2cm

Secure with tape.

6-7mm

Braid wire.

Triangle bead

String a bead on leftmost strand and braid wire. Repeat.

5.5cm
9 beads

Stop when you have reached desired length minus 0.5cm.

3. Make top of ring.

Pass wire through 8-mm plastic bead.

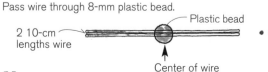

2 10-cm lengths wire

Plastic bead

Center of wire

Insert wire into ring made in Step 2.

Form a circle with round-nose pliers. Use needle-nose pliers to make spirals.

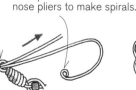

38

No. 45, 46 (p. 26)
Supplies

No. 45
(Decoration for glass candle holder)
Copper wire: 230cm 18-gauge silver wire, 3m 20-gauge silver wire
Beads: 5 x 10-mm oval designer beads with squared ends (6 white, 7 pink)

No. 46
(Decoration for glass candle holder)
Copper wire: 230cm 18-gauge brown wire, 3m 20-gauge brown wire
Beads: 8-mm fire-polished beads (6 topaz, 7 blue)

＊ *No. 45 and No. 46 differ in colors used only.*

Instructions for No. 45, 46

1. Make basketweave base.

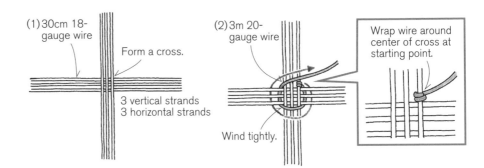

(1) 30cm 18-gauge wire
Form a cross.
3 vertical strands
3 horizontal strands

(2) 3m 20-gauge wire
Wind tightly.

Wrap wire around center of cross at starting point.

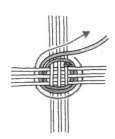

(3) Wind wire around center a second time.

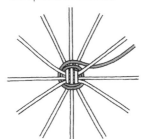

(4) Arrange the wires in the cross, forming a pattern resembling the spokes of a wheel.

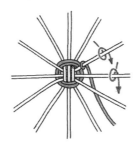

(5) Weave wire clockwise around the spokes, as shown below.

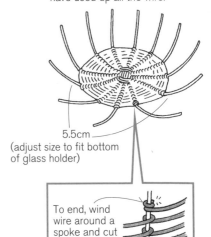

(6) When base is desired size, lay the glass holder on top of basketweave pattern. Continue weaving until you have used up all the wire.

5.5cm
(adjust size to fit bottom of glass holder)

To end, wind wire around a spoke and cut excess.

2. String beads, one at a time, onto spokes. Shape wire to fit glass holder.

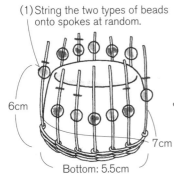

(1) String the two types of beads onto spokes at random.

6cm
7cm
Bottom: 5.5cm

(2) Cut spokes to varying lengths to achieve a nice balance. Form ends into flower shapes.

Round ends with round-nose pliers (see p. 42).

5mm

(3) Bend wire or form circles so that the beads will stay in place. Vary the height of the spokes.

3. Weave another row of wire around the spokes to hold them in place.

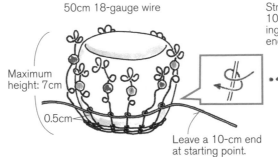

50cm 18-gauge wire

Maximum height: 7cm

0.5cm

Leave a 10-cm end at starting point.

String a bead onto the 10-cm wire left at starting point and shape end into a flower.

To end, wrap wire around spoke at starting point. Cut excess wire.

Supplies

No. 14 (Brooch)
Copper wire: 120cm 22-gauge natural wire
Beads: 6 3-mm gold-enameled pearl beads, 3-mm fire-polished beads (4 capri blue, 4 garnet), 4-mm fire-polished beads (2 amethyst, 3 olivine, 3 rose), 20-mm round blue Indian glass bead
Findings: 11.5-cm gold stickpin

No. 15 (Brooch)
Copper wire: 170cm 28-gauge copper wire
Beads: 1.6-mm Delica beads (75 pink (DB-104), 110 pale blue (DB-217)), 5-mm gold-enameled pearl bead
Findings: 15-mm perforated gold stickpin with chain

No. 16 (Brooch)
Copper wire: 520cm 28-gauge brown wire
Beads: 2-2.5-mm three-cut beads (391 red, 687 bronze)
Findings: 20-mm gold perforated pin back

Instructions for No. 16

1. Make small petals. *Arrangement of beads:* A: Red; make 5
B: Bronze; make 5
Total: 10 small petals

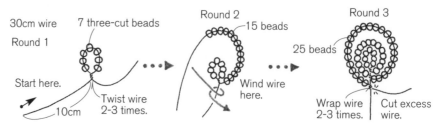

30cm wire
Round 1
Start here.
10cm
Twist wire 2-3 times.
7 three-cut beads
Round 2
15 beads
Wind wire here.
Round 3
25 beads
Wrap wire 2-3 times.
Cut excess wire.

2. Make large petals.

For Rounds 1-3, follow directions for small petals.

Arrangement of beads:
C: Bronze only; make 4
D: Red (Rounds 1, 2, 4; bronze (Round 3); make 2
E: Bronze (Rounds 1, 2, 4); red in (Round 3); make 1
F: Bronze (Rounds 1-3); red (Round 4); make 1
Total: 8 large petals

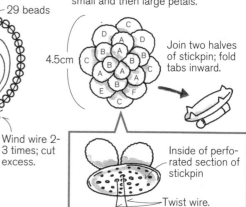

Round 4
29 beads
25
15
7
Wind wire 2-3 times; cut excess.

3. Attach brooch to stickpin.

Starting at center, attach small and then large petals.

4.5cm

Join two halves of stickpin; fold tabs inward.

Inside of perforated section of stickpin

Twist wire.

Instructions for No. 15

1. Make petals.

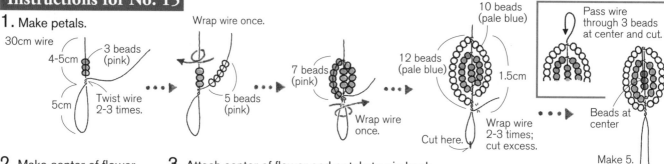

30cm wire
4-5cm
3 beads (pink)
5cm
Twist wire 2-3 times.
Wrap wire once.
5 beads (pink)
7 beads (pink)
Wrap wire once.
12 beads (pale blue)
Cut here.
10 beads (pale blue)
1.5cm
Wrap wire 2-3 times; cut excess.
Pass wire through 3 beads at center and cut.
Beads at center
Make 5.

2. Make center of flower.

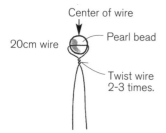

20cm wire
Center of wire
Pearl bead
Twist wire 2-3 times.

3. Attach center of flower and petals to pin back.

Attach center of flower in Round 1, and petals in Round 2.

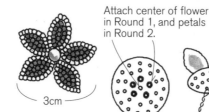

3cm

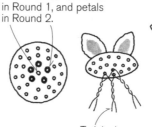

Twist wire on inside of pin back.

Join two halves of pin back and bend tabs.

(Instructions for No. 14 are on p. 41.)

1. Insert stickpin into Indian glass bead.

2. Wrap wire around pin.

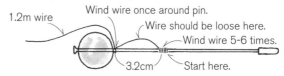

1.2m wire
Wind wire once around pin.
Wire should be loose here.
Wind wire 5-6 times.
3.2cm
Start here.

3. Pass wire through hole in bead and wrap around end of pin. Wind wire around bead while stringing smaller beads.

Wind wire once.

Pass wire through hole in bead.

String pearl and fire-polished beads at random while wrapping wire around Indian glass bead.

4. Wind wire around pin between base of Indian glass bead and starting point.

Wind wire around stickpin while stringing pearl and fire-polished beads at random.
Wind wire twice around base of Indian glass bead; cut excess.

String pearl and fire-polished beads at random while wrapping wire around Indian glass bead.

1. Glue plastic stones to all four surfaces of bottle.

Lay bottle on its side.

17cm

4cm

Arrange plastic stones, aiming for an attractive balance (8-12 stones on each surface).

Let glue dry before gluing next surface.

2. Make decoration for neck of bottle.

(1) 70cm wire

Bend at a 90° angle.

Bend at a 90° angle.

Needle-nose pliers

Leave a 3-5mm space between each turn of spiral.

(2) Make 3 square spirals in the same way.

1cm

1cm

(3) Attach spirals to neck of bottle.

3. Make more spirals, following directions in Step 2; wrap around bottle.

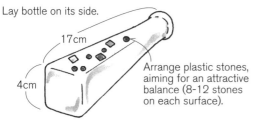

(1) 1
(2)
(3)
(4)
(5)
(6)
(7)
(8)

Make about 8 spirals in all.

2.5m wire

4. Secure spirals by wrapping a separate length of wire around bottle.

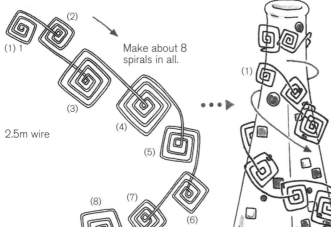

Wind wire here.

(1)

50cm wire

Wrap separate length of wire tightly around wire extending from spirals in several locations.

Round end of wire and attach to a square spiral.

No. 54, 55 (p. 31)
Supplies

No. 54 (Bottle decoration)
Copper wire: 370cm 18-gauge silver wire
Beads: Round plastic stones (2 each 5-mm, 9-mm, and 13-mm green; 14 5-mm pale blue, 2 9-mm yellow), 8 x 8-mm plastic stones (2 green, 3 pale blue, 4 yellow, 8 white)
Other supplies: Glue

No. 55 (Bottle decoration)
Copper wire: 5m 18-gauge silver wire
Beads: Fire-polished beads (5 5-mm emerald, 6 5-mm blue zircon, 7 8-mm blue)

(Instructions for No. 54 are on p. 41.)

Instructions for No. 55

1. Make spiral decoration.

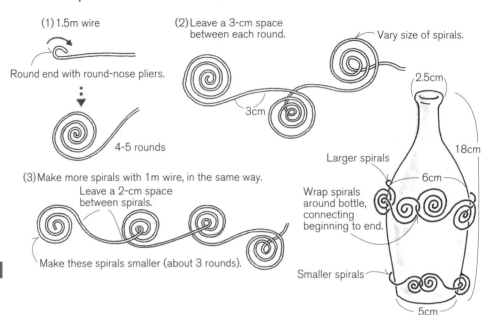

(1) 1.5m wire

Round end with round-nose pliers.

4-5 rounds

(2) Leave a 3-cm space between each round.

Vary size of spirals.

3cm

2.5cm

18cm

Larger spirals

6cm

Wrap spirals around bottle, connecting beginning to end.

Smaller spirals

5cm

(3) Make more spirals with 1m wire, in the same way. Leave a 2-cm space between spirals.

Make these spirals smaller (about 3 rounds).

2. Make flower decorations.

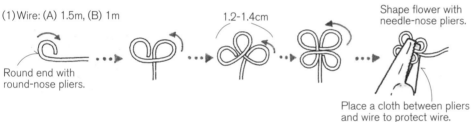

(1) Wire: (A) 1.5m, (B) 1m

Round end with round-nose pliers.

1.2-1.4cm

Shape flower with needle-nose pliers.

Place a cloth between pliers and wire to protect wire.

(2) Leave a 3-cm space between flowers.
Make one each of (A) and (B).

3cm

String beads at random.

3. Wind flowers around bottle.

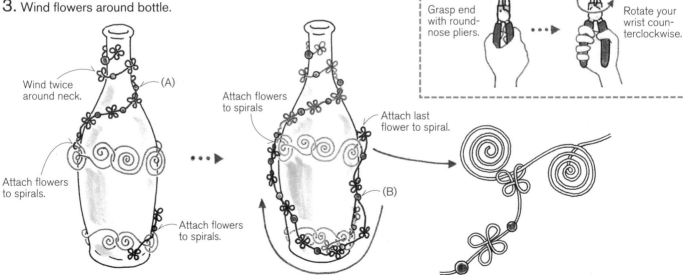

Wind twice around neck.

(A)

Attach flowers to spirals.

Attach flowers to spirals.

Attach flowers to spirals

Attach last flower to spiral.

(B)

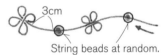

How to round the end of a wire

Grasp end with round-nose pliers.

Rotate your wrist counter-clockwise.

42

No. 47, 48 (p. 27)
Supplies

No. 47 (Jewelry or card stand)
Copper wire: 60cm 18-gauge black wire
Beads: 4-mm cube beads (10 purple, 10 yellow, 14 yellow-green)
Other supplies: 1 package anthracite Fimo Soft, glue

No. 48 (Jewelry or card stand)
Copper wire: 60cm 18-gauge black wire
Beads: 4-mm cube beads (10 red, 26 black, 26 white)
Other supplies: 1 package white Fimo Soft, glue

Instructions for No. 47, 48

1. Make the base by shaping Fimo into a cube.

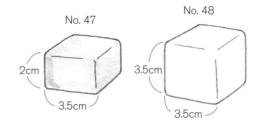

No. 47

No. 48

2cm
3.5cm

3.5cm
3.5cm

2. Press beads into base.

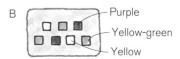

No. 47

A — Yellow — Yellow-green — Purple

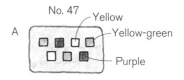

B — Purple — Yellow-green — Yellow

No. 48

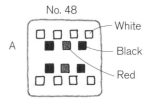

A — White — Black — Red

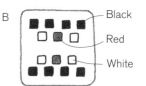

B — Black — Red — White

3. Use wire to make a hole at center of upper surface. Bake for about 20 minutes in a 120° C (265° F) oven.

Make a 3-mm hole here.

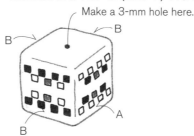

B
B
A
B

4. Make upper section of stand.

30cm wire

12cm

Make a 12-cm spiral, starting at one end.

3cm

Make 2.

3.2cm
6.8cm
Twist wire once to join.

Twist wire as you string the beads.

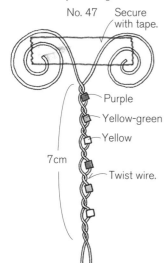

No. 47
Secure with tape.

Purple
Yellow-green
Yellow
7cm
Twist wire.

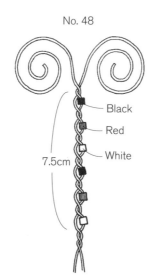

No. 48

Black
Red
White
7.5cm

5. Insert wire into hole in base and glue to secure.

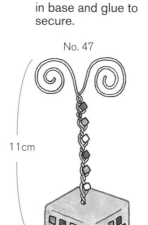

No. 47

11cm

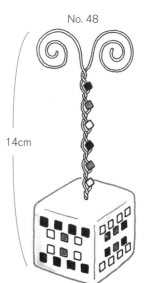

No. 48

14cm

No. 49 (p. 28)
Supplies

No. 49 (Mini-rack)

Copper wire: Silver (260cm 18-gauge wire, 2m 20-gauge wire, 15m 28-gauge wire)

Beads: 8 8-mm blue fire-polished beads, 2.5-mm triangle beads (115 gray, 352 pale blue), 2-2.5-mm three-cut beads (228 blue, 265 white, 695 yellow-green, 1,011 purple)

Instructions for No. 49

1. Make framework.

50cm 18-gauge wire

Round one end of wire twice with round-nose pliers.

4mm

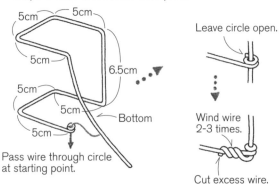

Shape corners with needle-nose pliers.

5cm 5cm
5cm 6.5cm
5cm
5cm 5cm
Bottom

Pass wire through circle at starting point.

Leave circle open.

Wind wire 2-3 times.

Cut excess wire.

2. Make door.

11cm 18-gauge wire

(1) Round one end of wire twice (2cm) with round-nose pliers.

4mm
6.5cm
(2) Cut here.
2cm

6.5cm

Round other end of wire (2cm).

(2) Bend 30cm 18-gauge wire as shown below.

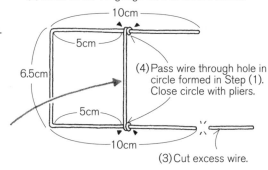

10cm
5cm
6.5cm
5cm
10cm

(4) Pass wire through hole in circle formed in Step (1). Close circle with pliers.

(3) Cut excess wire.

3. Make uprights.

20cm 18-gauge wire

Bend with pliers.

5cm

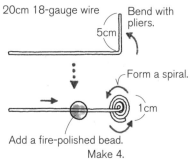

Form a spiral.

1cm

Add a fire-polished bead.
Make 4.

4. Weave bottom (see p. 39 for instructions).

Spoke 6 15-cm lengths 18-gauge wire

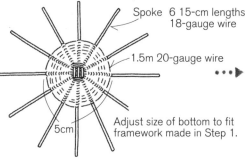

1.5m 20-gauge wire

5cm

Adjust size of bottom to fit framework made in Step 1.

Cut wire on all but the two center spokes, leaving 0.5-cm ends.

Wrong side

Bend over to wrong side.

Round ends of wire twice.

5cm

5cm

5. Assemble framework, bottom and uprights.

(1) Insert uprights into circles on bottom.

Right side

(2) Attach framework.

Wrap uprights once around framework.

Insert uprights into circles in framework and secure.

Framework   Upright

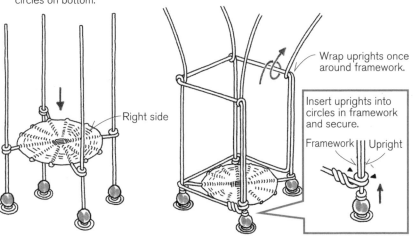

6. Attach door.

Wrap wire loosely around framework and upright twice.

Door

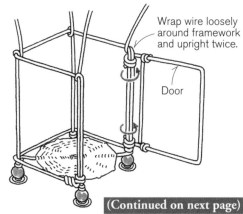

(Continued on next page)

7. Attach decorations to uprights.

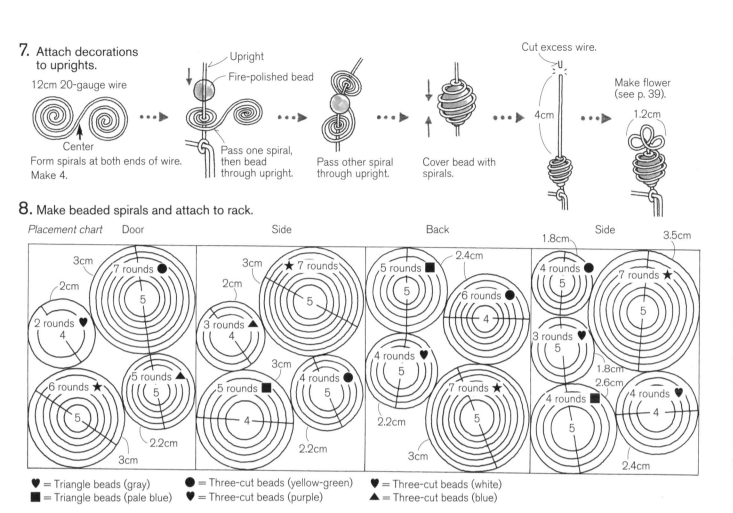

12cm 20-gauge wire

Center

Form spirals at both ends of wire.
Make 4.

Upright
Fire-polished bead

Pass one spiral, then bead through upright.

Pass other spiral through upright.

Cover bead with spirals.

Cut excess wire.

4cm

Make flower (see p. 39).

1.2cm

8. Make beaded spirals and attach to rack.

Placement chart

Door

3cm
2cm
7 rounds ●
5
2 rounds ♥
4
6 rounds ★
5
5 rounds ▲
5
2.2cm
3cm

Side

3cm
2cm
★ 7 rounds
5
3 rounds ▲
4
5 rounds ■
4
3cm
4 rounds ●
5
2.2cm
2.2cm

Back

5 rounds ■
5
2.4cm
6 rounds ●
4
4 rounds ♥
5
7 rounds ★
5
2.2cm
3cm

Side

1.8cm
3.5cm
4 rounds ●
5
7 rounds ★
5
3 rounds ♥
5
1.8cm
2.6cm
4 rounds ■
5
4 rounds ♥
4
2.4cm

♥ = Triangle beads (gray)
■ = Triangle beads (pale blue)
● = Three-cut beads (yellow-green)
♥ = Three-cut beads (purple)
♥ = Three-cut beads (white)
▲ = Three-cut beads (blue)

(1) Make beaded spirals.
(Instructions for stringing beads are on p. 40.)

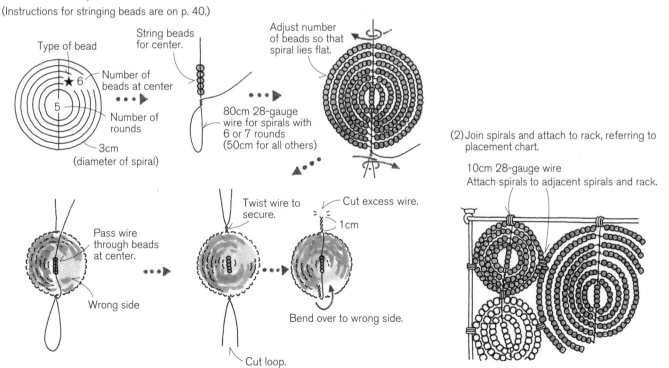

Type of bead
Number of beads at center
★ 6
5
Number of rounds
3cm
(diameter of spiral)

String beads for center.

Adjust number of beads so that spiral lies flat.

80cm 28-gauge wire for spirals with 6 or 7 rounds (50cm for all others)

Pass wire through beads at center.

Wrong side

Twist wire to secure.

Cut excess wire.

1cm

Bend over to wrong side.

Cut loop.

(2) Join spirals and attach to rack, referring to placement chart.

10cm 28-gauge wire
Attach spirals to adjacent spirals and rack.

No. 50 (p. 29)
Supplies

No. 50 (Glass decoration)

Copper wire: 28 gauge wire (1m magenta, 4m brown, 5m silver, 10m aqua, 13m natural, 31m green)

Beads: 2-2.5-mm three-cut beads (330 yellow-green, 495 blue, 495 purple, 495 beige, 2,640 white), 2-mm seed beads (372 green, 496 yellow-green), 2.5-mm triangle beads (190 navy, 285 yellow-green, 285 dark green, 380 blue, 760 green), 253 6-mm white bugle beads

Instructions for No. 50

1. Make netted section for stem of glass; attach to glass.

(1) Make netting.

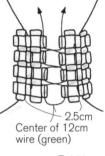

(2) Wrap around stem of glass and join.

Bugle bead
Row 1
Row 2
Row 8
4 squares
Form intersections.
Start here.
Center of 1.5m wire (green)
Repeat for a total of 8 rows (adjust to fit glass used).
Twist wire to secure; bend over to wrong side.
2.5cm
Center of 12cm wire (green)

: Twist to secure; bend over to wrong side.

2. Make netting for sides of glass; wrap around glass.

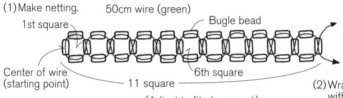

(1) Make netting.
50cm wire (green)
1st square
Bugle bead
Center of wire (starting point)
6th square
11 square
(Adjust to fit glass used.)

(2) Wrap netting around glass; join with same strand of wire.

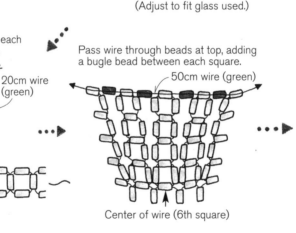

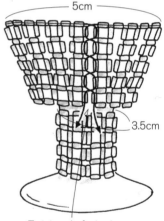

Add four squares to each of the 11 first made.

Twist wire at end to secure.
Bend over to wrong side.
20cm wire (green)
Center of wire (starting point)

Pass wire through beads at top, adding a bugle bead between each square.
50cm wire (green)
Center of wire (6th square)

5cm
3.5cm
Twist end of wire to secure; bend over to wrong side.

3. Make leaves.

(Instructions for stringing beads are on p. 40.)

Three-cut beads

26 22 18 13 10 5 7 10 14 18 22

Colors of beads and wire

Beads: white
 Wire: green (13 leaves); natural, silver, aqua (1 leaf each)

Beads: beige
 Wire: brown, magenta, aqua (1 leaf each)

Beads: purple
 Wire: natural, green, aqua (1 leaf each)

Beads: yellow-green
 Wire: natural, aqua (1 leaf each)

Beads: blue
 Wire: green, silver, aqua (1 leaf each)

＊Use 1m wire for all leaves.

(Continued on next page)

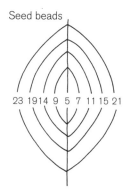

Seed beads

23 19 14 9 5 7 11 15 21

Colors of beads and wire

Beads: yellow-green
Wire: natural, green, silver, aqua (1 leaf each)

Beads: green
Wire: natural, brown,
green (1 leaf each)

＊Use 1m wire for all
leaves.

Triangle beads

17 14 10 6 5 6 9 12 16

Colors of beads and wire

Beads: green
Wire: green (5 leaves);
natural, silver, aqua
(1 leaf each)

Beads: yellow-green
Wire: natural, green,
aqua (1 leaf each)

＊Use 1m wire for all
leaves.

Beads: dark green
Wire: natural, green,
aqua (1 leaf each)

Beads: blue
Wire: natural, green, silver, aqua (1 leaf each)

Beads: navy
Wire: brown (2 leaves)

4. Attach leaves to netting.

(1) Begin at stem of glass.

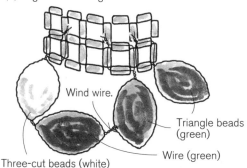

Wind wire.

Triangle beads
(green)

Wire (green)

Three-cut beads (white)
Wire (green)

(2) Attach leaves, one by one, until netting is covered.

Triangle beads (yellow-green)
Wire (aqua): 1 leaf
Three-cut beads (white)
Wire (green): Set aside 11 leaves.

Attach remainder at random.

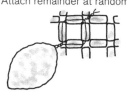

(3) Turn glass over, rearrange
leaves, and secure with wire.

10cm wire
(natural)

Join overlapping
leaves at tip.

Twist wire to secure;
hide behind leaf.

5. Attach decoration to mouth of glass.

(1) Join remaining 11 leaves.

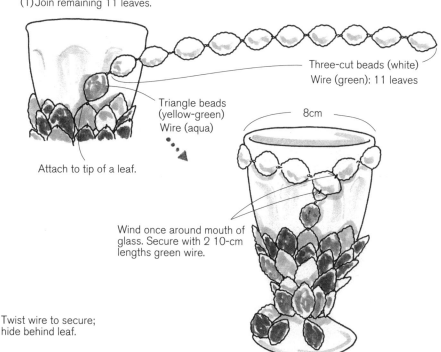

Three-cut beads (white)
Wire (green): 11 leaves

Triangle beads
(yellow-green)
Wire (aqua)

Attach to tip of a leaf.

8cm

Wind once around mouth of
glass. Secure with 2 10-cm
lengths green wire.

No. 51, 52, 53
(p. 30)
Supplies

No. 51
(Decoration for glass candle holder)
Copper wire: 65cm 20-gauge silver wire, 120cm 18-gauge silver wire
Beads: 3-mm seed beads (5 orange, 13 silver, 21 red)

No. 52
(Decoration for glass candle holder)
Copper wire: 65cm 20-gauge silver wire, 120cm 18-gauge silver wire
Beads: 3-mm seed beads (5 pale blue, 13 silver, 21 blue)

No. 53
(Decoration for glass candle holder)
Copper wire: 65cm 20-gauge silver wire, 120cm 18-gauge silver wire
Beads: 3-mm seed beads (5 yellow-green, 13 silver, 21 green)

* *No. 51, 52 and No. 53 differ in colors used only.*

Instructions for No. 51, 52, 53

1. Make garland.

(1) Make flowers.

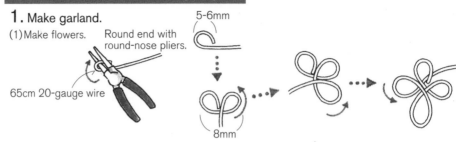

Round end with round-nose pliers.

65cm 20-gauge wire

5-6mm

8mm

(2) String beads; twist wire to secure.

Seed bead

Red (No. 51), blue (No. 52), green (No. 53)

Form a circle.

1cm

Orange (No. 51)
Pale blue (No. 52)
Yellow-green (No. 53)

Silver bead

1cm   1cm

Alternate orientation of circles.

⌞—— A ——⌟⌜—— B ——⌟

(3) Make flowers in the following order: A-B-A-B-A, adjusting for diameter of mouth of glass. Wrap flowers around glass, attaching first flower to last. Cut excess wire.

Compress with pliers; cut excess wire.

2. Make spirals and attach to glass.

30cm 18-gauge wire

⌜— 10cm —⌝

Use 10cm wire for each spiral.

1.4cm

Orange (No. 51)
Blue (No. 52)
Green (No. 53)

String beads on wire.   Silver beads

Form a 10-cm spiral at other end. Make four of these sections.

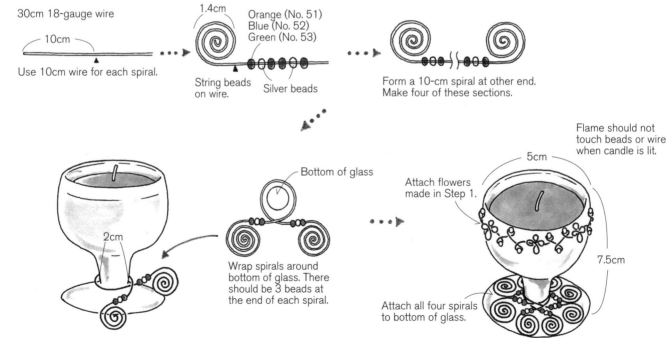

2cm

Bottom of glass

Wrap spirals around bottom of glass. There should be 3 beads at the end of each spiral.

Flame should not touch beads or wire when candle is lit.

5cm

Attach flowers made in Step 1.

7.5cm

Attach all four spirals to bottom of glass.

No. 23 (p. 13)

Tools and Supplies

WigJig Delphi (see p. 10 for instructions)

No. 23 (Chain belt)

Copper wire: 350cm 28-gauge copper wire, 720cm 18-gauge copper wire

Beads: 2.5-mm triangle beads (16 purple, 20 pale blue), 20 2-mm yellow-green seed beads, 14 4-mm amethyst fire-polished beads

Instructions for No. 23

1. Make sections of belt measuring 6mm in diameter.

18-gauge wire

(1) Make coils from wire.

Use round-nose pliers.

Wrap wire around widest part of pliers.

Use about 650cm wire.

Or use the Wire Worker (see p. 22).

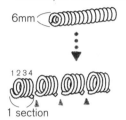

(2) Cut each coil into four sections, for a total of 66.

6mm

1 2 3 4

1 section

Cut coil.

(3) Bend coil down at each end.

3. Make butterfly decorations.

(1) Make two butterflies, using WigJig Delphi.

Peg placement

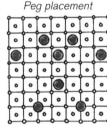

25cm 18-gauge wire

Start here.   End here.

(1) (6)

(3)

(4)

3.8cm

(5)

(2)

3.4cm

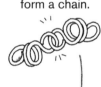

2. Connect sections made in Step 1 to form a chain.

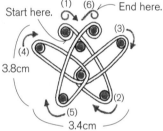

(2) String beads while winding wire.

160cm 28-gauge wire

Wind wire tightly.

Start here.

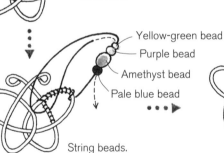

Yellow-green bead
Purple bead
Amethyst bead
Pale blue bead

String beads.

Continue stringing beads in the same way.

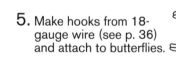

Length: 1m

Wrap adjoining sections of wire tightly.

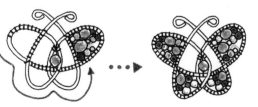

5. Make hooks from 18-gauge wire (see p. 36) and attach to butterflies.

4. Attach butterflies.

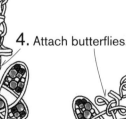

No. 17, 18, 19
(p. 11)

Tools and Supplies

WigJig Delphi (see p. 10 for instructions)

No. 17 (Necklace)

Copper wire: 3m 20-gauge silver wire
Beads: 9 6-mm capri blue fire-polished beads
Findings: Silver clasp set with adjustable chain closure

No. 18 (Bracelet)

Copper wire: 420cm 20-gauge silver wire
Beads: Capri blue fire-polished beads (18 3-mm beads, 10 6-mm beads)
Findings: Silver bracelet clasp set

No. 19 (Ring)

Copper wire: 60cm 20-gauge silver wire
Beads: 6-mm capri blue fire-polished bead

Instructions for No. 17

1. Use WigJig Delphi to make 7 motifs.

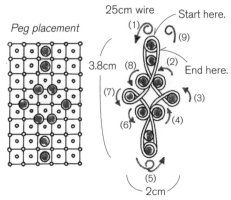

Peg placement

25cm wire

Start here. (1)

(9)

3.8cm (8) (2) End here.

(7) (3)

(6) (4)

(5)

2cm

Form circles at beginning and end of motif.

2. Make 8 spirals.

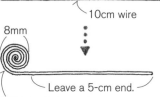

(1) Round end with round-nose pliers. Leave enough space for wire to pass through.

10cm wire

8mm

Leave a 5-cm end.

(2) Make 3-4 rounds.

(3) Make a spiral facing opposite direction from remaining 5cm wire.

3. Wind spirals made in Step 2 around beads.

(1) Round end with round-nose pliers.

5cm wire

(2) Pass wire through one of the spirals made in Step 2.

(3) String a bead onto wire.

(4) Pass wire through other spiral.

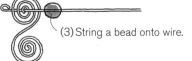

(6) Cut wire, leaving a 9-mm end; round end.

(5) Wrap spiral around bead.

Make 8 of these sections.

Center round of spiral

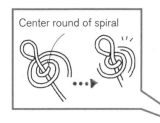

6. Attach findings.

Adjustable chain closure

Jump ring
(Instructions for opening jump rings are on p. 37.)

Clasp

Length: 36cm (excluding adjustable chain closure)

5. Join spiral-covered beads and motifs.

4. Attach bead to motif at center of necklace.

(1) Round end of wire with round-nose pliers.

5cm wire

(3) Cut excess wire; round end.

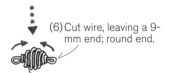

(2) Insert wire into bead.

(Instructions for No. 18, 19 are on next page.)

Instructions for No. 18

(Instructions for motifs and spiral-covered beads are on p. 50.)

1. Make 10.

2, 3. Make 6 using 6-mm beads.

5. Make 18 using 5cm wire and 3-mm beads (follow instructions in Step 4).

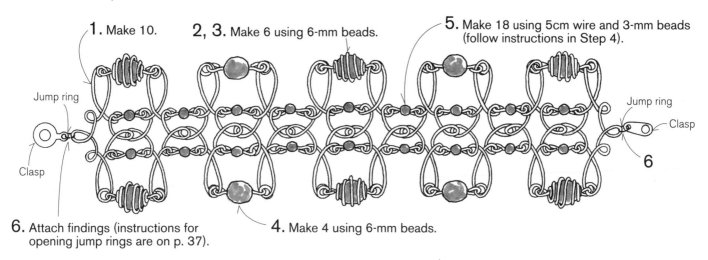

Jump ring

Clasp

Jump ring

Clasp

6

6. Attach findings (instructions for opening jump rings are on p. 37).

4. Make 4 using 6-mm beads.

Instructions for No. 19

1. Make 1 motif, following instructions in Step 1 of No. 17 (p. 50).

2. Follow instructions in Step 4 of No. 17 to complete motif.

4. Place motif over pattern and shape.

3. Make a pattern with a diameter equivalent to desired finished size by wrapping a piece of paper around a pen or similar object.

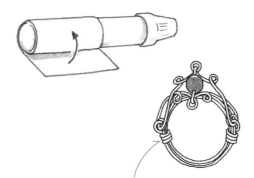

6. Wrap wire around band; cut excess.

5. Wind wire around pattern; attach motif.

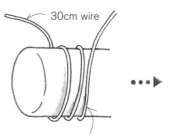

30cm wire

(2) Place motif on top of band.

(1) Wrap wire around pattern (two-and-a-half turns).

(3) Pass wire through holes in motif. Remove ring from pattern.

51

No. 20, 21, 22
(p. 12)
Tools and Supplies

WigJig Delphi (see p. 10 for instructions)

No. 20 (Necklace)

Copper wire: 450cm 20-gauge brown wire

Beads: 4-mm fire-polished beads (10 royal blue, 10 sapphire), 10 5-mm bronze fire-polished beads, 6 6-mm capri blue fire-polished beads

No. 21 (Bracelet)

Copper wire: 2m 20-gauge brown wire

Beads: 4-mm fire-polished beads (6 royal blue, 6 sapphire), 6 5-mm bronze fire-polished beads, 3 6-mm capri blue fire-polished beads

No. 22 (Earrings)

Copper wire: 1m 20-gauge brown wire

Beads: 4-mm fire-polished beads (2 sapphire, 4 royal blue), 2 5-mm bronze fire-polished beads

Instructions for No. 20

1. Use WigJig Delphi to make 18 motifs.

Peg placement

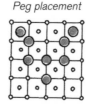

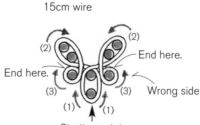

15cm wire

End here.

End here.

(2)   (2)

(3)   (3)

Wrong side

(1)   (1)

Starting point (center of wire)

2. String beads on wire; insert into motif.

Bend end of wire with round-nose pliers.

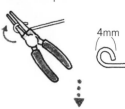

4mm

2cm wire

Bronze bead

Make 10.

4cm wire

Sapphire bead

Royal blue bead

Capri blue bead

Make 5.

3. Make 16 jump rings.

Wrap 50cm wire around nose of pliers.

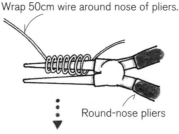

Round-nose pliers

Cut with wire-cutter.

Wrap 23 times.

3mm

Make 5.

4. Join motifs made in Steps 1 and 2 with jump rings (instructions for opening jump rings areon p. 37).

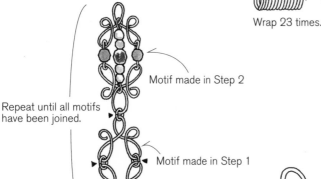

Repeat until all motifs have been joined.

Motif made in Step 2

Motif made in Step 1

Jump ring made in Step 3

5. Make jump rings for adjustable chain closure. Follow instructions in Step 3.

6mm

4mm

Make 7 of each using 20cm wire.

(Continued on next page)

Length: 37cm (excluding adjustable chain closure)

6mm

4mm

6. Join jump rings made in Step 5, alternating between 4-mm and 6-mm rings.

7. Make decoration for adjustable chain closure.

5cm wire
3-4mm

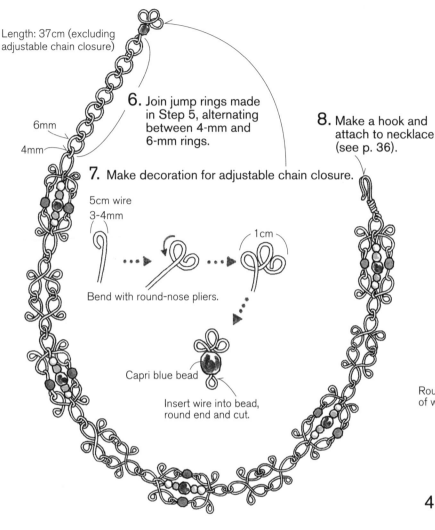

Bend with round-nose pliers.

1cm

Capri blue bead

Insert wire into bead, round end and cut.

8. Make a hook and attach to necklace (see p. 36).

(see p. 36)

1. Make 2 motifs, following instructions for No. 20 on p. 52.

No. 20 on p. 52

2. String beads on wire.

5cm wire

Bend into a loop.

Bead (make 4 with royal blue and 2 with sapphire beads)

4mm

Make 2-3-round spirals with round-nose pliers.

2cm wire

Round ends of wire.

Bronze bead (make 2)

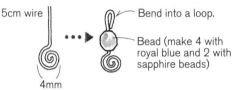

4. Make ear wires and attach.

(Actual size)

3. Join sections made in Step 2 to motif.

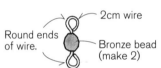

Instructions for No. 21

1. Make motifs, following instructions for No. 20 on p. 52.

No. 20 on p. 52

Make 3.

Make 2.

2. Make 4 jump rings, following instructions for No. 20 on p. 52. Use them to join motifs made in Step 1.

No. 20 on p. 52

(Instructions for opening jump rings are on p. 37.)

(Instructions for opening jump rings are on p. 37.)

3mm

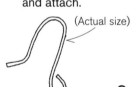

Close ring.

3. Make hooks and attach (see p. 36).

(see p. 36)

No. 44 (p. 25)

Tools and Supplies

WigJig Delphi (see p. 10 for instructions)

No. 44 (Decorated photo frame)

Copper wire: 220cm each natural and copper 22-gauge wire, 120cm natural and 14m copper 28-gauge wire

Beads: Fire-polished beads (8 4-mm amethyst, 4 6-mm purple), 2.5-mm triangle beads (88 pale blue, 96 purple), 144 2-mm yellow-green seed beads

Other supplies: Glue

Instructions for No. 44

1. Use WigJig Delphi to make flower motifs.

(1) Make Motif A.

Make 6 each with 22-gauge natural and copper wire.

Peg placement

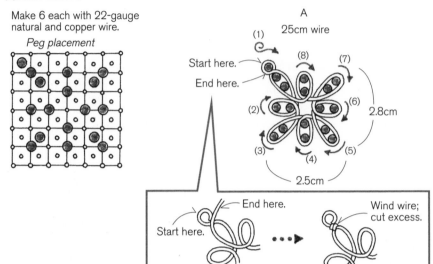

(2) Make Motif B.

Make 2 each with 22-gauge natural and copper wire.

Peg placement

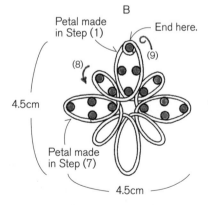

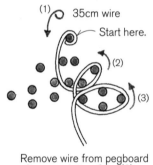

Remove wire from pegboard after completing Step (3).

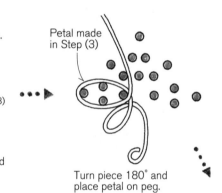

Turn piece 180° and place petal on peg.

Make Petals (4)-(7). Remove wire from pegboard.

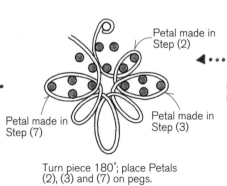

Turn piece 180°; place Petals (2), (3) and (7) on pegs.

Use natural wire only. Finish beginning and end of motif, as shown below.

 Wind 20cm 28-gauge natural wire around beginning and end.

54

(Continued on next page)

2. Add beads to Motifs A and B.

A: 6 copper beads
B: 2 copper beads

20cm wire = length of 1 petal

Use 8 20-cm lengths wire for each motif.

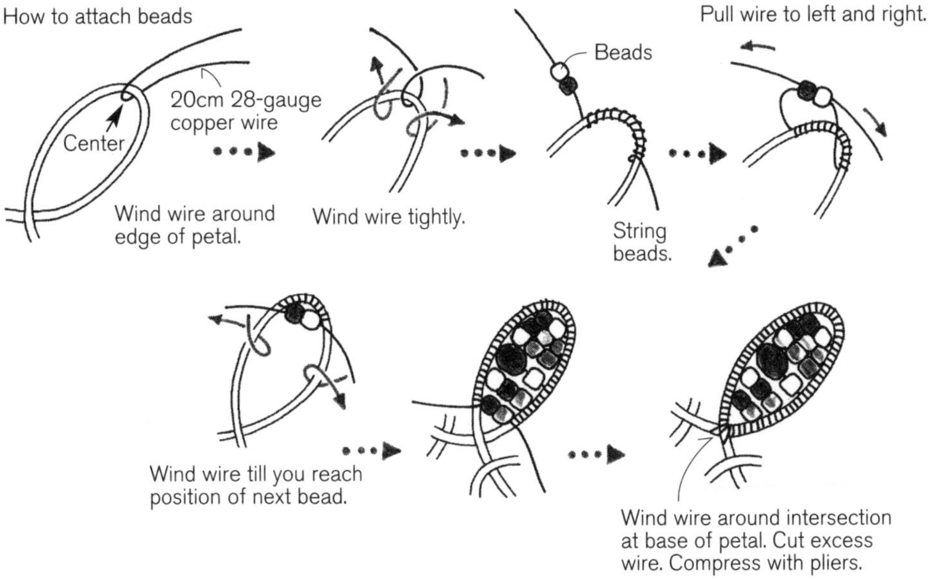

How to attach beads
Center
20cm 28-gauge copper wire
Wind wire around edge of petal.
Wind wire tightly.
Beads
String beads.
Pull wire to left and right.
Wind wire till you reach position of next bead.
Wind wire around intersection at base of petal. Cut excess wire. Compress with pliers.

Bead placement (Actual size)

A': Make 6.

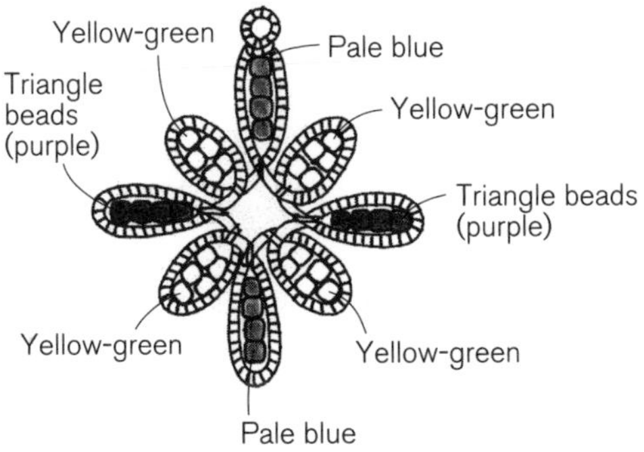

Yellow-green
Pale blue
Triangle beads (purple)
Yellow-green
Triangle beads (purple)
Yellow-green
Yellow-green
Pale blue

B': Make 2.

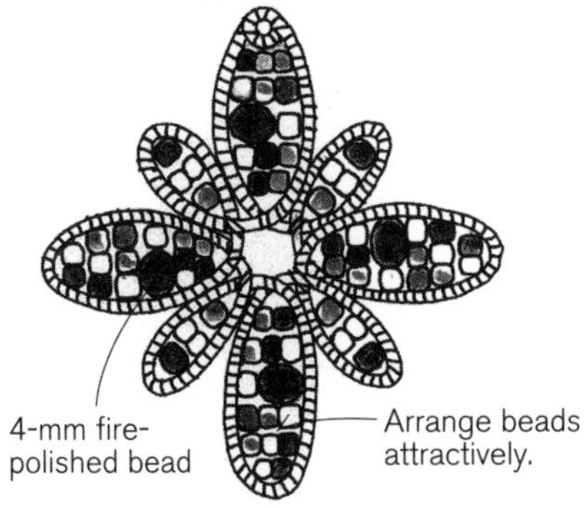

4-mm fire-polished bead
Arrange beads attractively.

5. Connect first petals in adjacent A motifs with 20cm 28-gauge natural wire. Wrap wire as shown below.

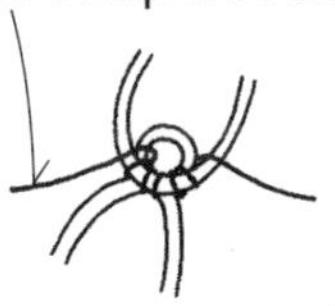

※Glue motifs to frame, making adjustments if your frame is a different size.

4. Join a B motif and 2 A' motifs with 28-gauge natural wire in the same way.

6. Place an A' motif on an A motif and join. Use 20cm 28-gauge copper wire.

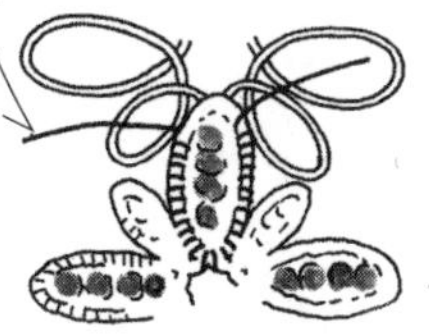

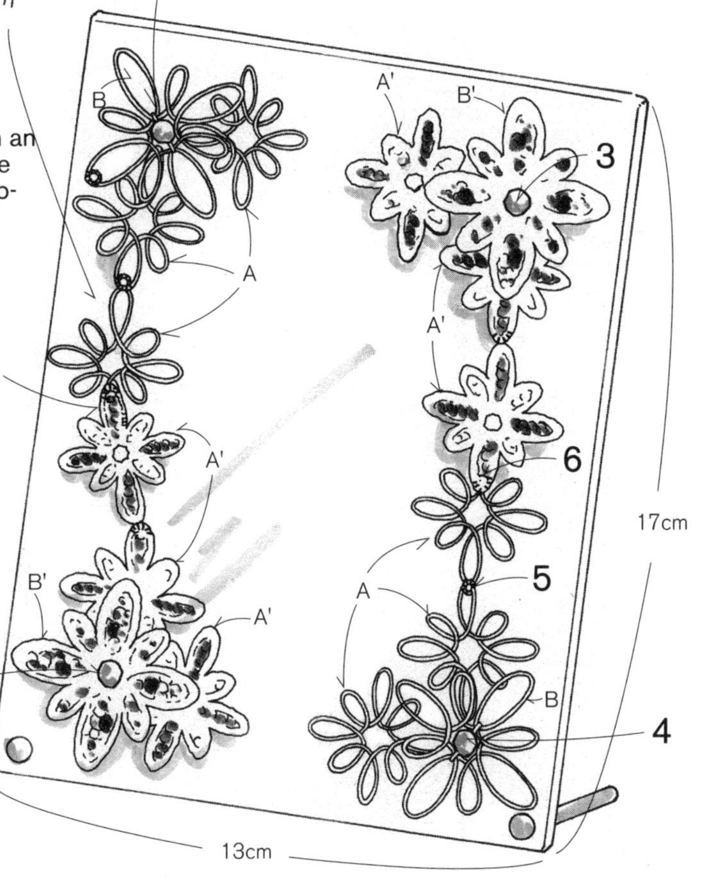

B
A'
B'
3
A
A'
A'
6
17cm
B'
A'
A
5
B
4
13cm

3. Join a B motif to 2 A' motifs.

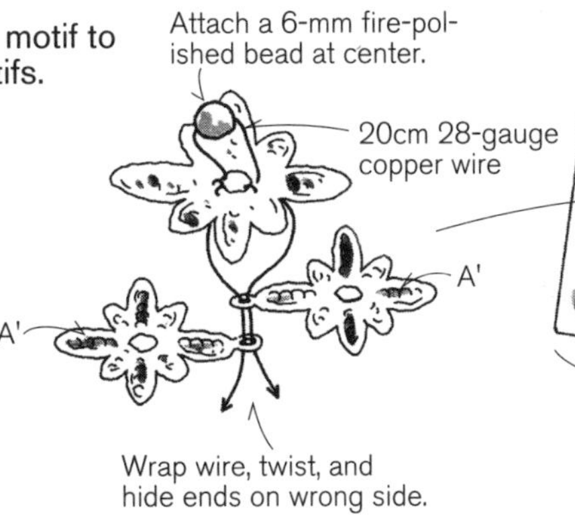

Attach a 6-mm fire-polished bead at center.
20cm 28-gauge copper wire
A'
A'
Wrap wire, twist, and hide ends on wrong side.

No. 24, 25 (p. 14)
Tools and Supplies

WigJig Delphi (see p. 10 for instructions)

No. 24 (Necklace)
Copper wire: 187cm 18-gauge black wire, 520cm 28-gauge black wire
Beads: 8 8-mm blue fire-polished beads, 8 5-mm round purple designer beads

No. 25 (Necklace)
Copper wire: 187cm 18-gauge silver wire, 520cm 28-gauge silver wire
Beads: 8 8-mm pale blue fire-polished beads, 8 4-mm peridot cat's-eye beads

---

∗ No. 24 and No. 25 differ in colors used only.

Instructions for No. 24, 25

1. Use WigJig Delphi to make 15 motifs.

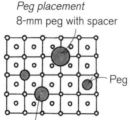

Peg placement
8-mm peg with spacer

Peg

5-mm peg with spacer

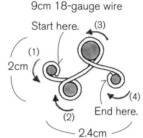

9cm 18-gauge wire

Start here.

(1) (2) (3) (4)

2cm

2.4cm

End here.

Attach 1 bead to each motif.

2. String a bead on 18-gauge wire while winding wire around motif.

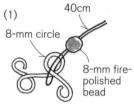

(1)

40cm

8-mm circle

8-mm fire-polished bead

Loop wire around center before stringing bead.

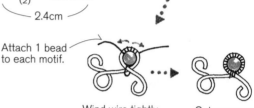

Wind wire tightly, working to left and right from center.

Cut excess wire. Make 7.

(2)

No. 24: 5-mm designer beads
No. 25: 4-mm cat's-eye beads

Bead

5-mm circle

Wind wire, following instructions in Step (1). Make 8.

5. Make an adjustable chain closure and attach to necklace.

Make 7 jump rings with 15cm 18-gauge wire (see p. 52).

7mm

4. Make a hook and attach to end of necklace (see p. 36).

Length: 34cm (excluding adjustable chain closure)

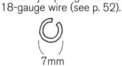

6. Make decoration for adjustable chain closure and attach.

Round end of 2.5cm 18-gauge wire with round-nose pliers.

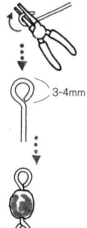

3-4mm

Insert wire into bead; round other end of wire.

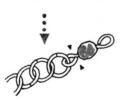

Attach to adjustable chain closure.

3. Make jump rings for connecting the motifs.

Join motifs made in Steps (1) and (2) in alternation. Make 14 jump rings using 25cm 18-gauge wire. (Instructions for opening jump rings are on p. 37.)

 (See p. 52.)

4-5mm

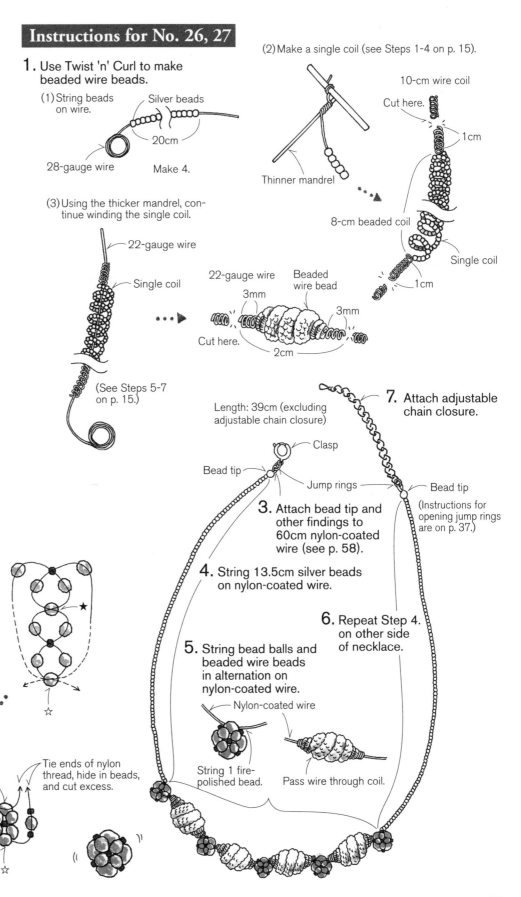

No. 26, 27 (p. 16)
Tools and Supplies
Twist 'n' Curl (see p. 15 for instructions)

No. 26 (Necklace)
Copper wire: 120cm 22-gauge silver wire, 4m 28-gauge white wire
Beads: 1.5-mm seed beads (30 purple, 1,102 silver), 60 3-mm amethyst fire-polished beads
Other supplies: Silver clasp set with adjustable chain closure, 250cm No. 2 (0.24mm) clear nylon wire, 60cm clear 0.36-mm nylon-coated wire, 2 silver crimp beads

No. 27 (Necklace)
Copper wire: 120cm 22-gauge silver wire, 4m 28-gauge white wire
Beads: 1,132 1.5-mm silver seed beads, 60 3-mm aqua fire-polished beads,
Other supplies: Silver clasp set with adjustable chain closure, 250cm No. 2 (0.24mm) clear nylon thread, 60cm 0.36-mm clear nylon-coated wire, 2 silver crimp beads

∗ No. 26 and No. 27 differ in colors used only.

Instructions for No. 26, 27

1. Use Twist 'n' Curl to make beaded wire beads.

(1) String beads on wire.
Silver beads
20cm
28-gauge wire
Make 4.

(2) Make a single coil (see Steps 1-4 on p. 15).
Thinner mandrel
10-cm wire coil
Cut here.
1cm
8-cm beaded coil
Single coil
1cm

(3) Using the thicker mandrel, continue winding the single coil.
22-gauge wire
Single coil
(See Steps 5-7 on p. 15.)

22-gauge wire
Beaded wire bead
3mm
3mm
Cut here.
2cm

2. Make a bead ball.
1.5mm seed beads
No. 26: Purple
No. 27: Silver
Fire-polished beads
50cm nylon thread
Start here.
★
☆
Pull nylon thread to shape ball.
Tie ends of nylon thread, hide in beads, and cut excess.
★
☆

3. Attach bead tip and other findings to 60cm nylon-coated wire (see p. 58).

4. String 13.5cm silver beads on nylon-coated wire.

5. String bead balls and beaded wire beads in alternation on nylon-coated wire.
Nylon-coated wire
String 1 fire-polished bead.
Pass wire through coil.

6. Repeat Step 4. on other side of necklace.

7. Attach adjustable chain closure.

Length: 39cm (excluding adjustable chain closure)
Clasp
Bead tip
Jump rings
Bead tip
(Instructions for opening jump rings are on p. 37.)

57

No. 28, 29 (p. 17)
Tools and Supplies

Twist 'n' Curl (see p. 15 for instructions)

No. 28 (Choker)

Copper wire: 7m 20-gauge black wire, 250cm 22-gauge silver wire, 7m 28-gauge silver wire

Beads: Fire-polished beads (15 3-mm jet black, 18 6-mm garnet), 1.5-mm seed beads (460 black, 1,932 silver)

Other supplies: 4 silver bead tips, silver spring clasp, silver adjustable chain closure, 1m 0.36mm clear nylon-coated wire, 4 silver crimp beads

No. 29 (Choker)

Copper wire: 70cm 20-gauge black wire, 250cm 22-gauge black wire, 7m 28-gauge dark blue wire

Beads: Fire-polished beads (20 3-mm hematite, 18 6-mm capri blue), 1.5-mm seed beads (460 black, 1,932 navy)

Other supplies: 4 silver bead tips, silver spring clasp, silver adjustable chain closure, 1m 0.36mm clear nylon-coated wire, 4 silver crimp beads

* *No. 28 and No. 29 differ in colors used only.*

Instructions for No. 28, 29

1. Use Twist 'n' Curl to make 7 beaded wire beads (see instructions on p. 57).

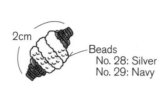

2cm

Beads
No. 28: Silver
No. 29: Navy

3. Attach bead tip to nylon-coated wire.

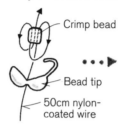

Crimp bead

Bead tip

50cm nylon-coated wire

2. Finish beads made in Step 1.

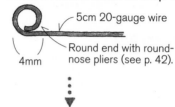

5cm 20-gauge wire

Round end with round-nose pliers (see p. 42).

4mm

Insert wire into beaded wire bead.

Cut wire, leaving a 1-cm end. Round end with round-nose pliers.

3cm

Make 7 of the same length.

Compress crimp bead with pliers; cut excess wire.

Close bead tip; round end.

7. Make decorations for ends of choker.

Round end with round-nose pliers

4mm

1.2cm

6-mm fire-polished bead

4mm

5cm 20-gauge wire

6. Attach bead tips to beaded wire beads.

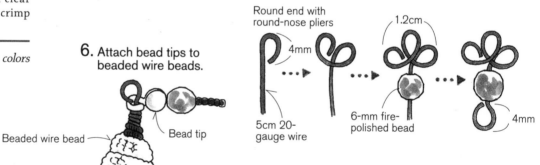

Beaded wire bead

Bead tip

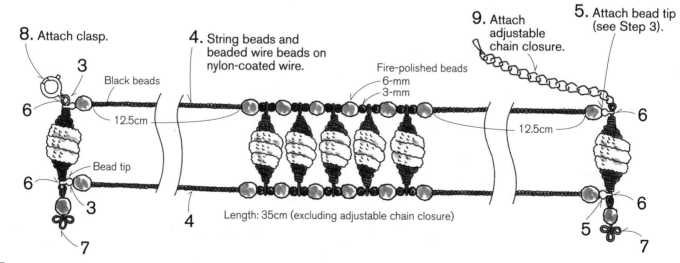

8. Attach clasp.

3

Black beads

6

12.5cm

Bead tip

6

3

4. String beads and beaded wire beads on nylon-coated wire.

4

Fire-polished beads
6-mm
3-mm

9. Attach adjustable chain closure.

5. Attach bead tip (see Step 3).

12.5cm

6

6

5

7

Length: 35cm (excluding adjustable chain closure)

No. 30, 31 (p. 18)

Tools and Supplies

Twist 'n' Curl (see p. 15 for instructions)

No. 30 (Necklace)

Copper wire: 350cm 22-gauge natural wire, 840cm 28-gauge natural wire

Beads: Round pink designer beads (1 5-mm, 18 8-mm) 6 6 x 10-mm oval green designer beads with squared ends, 438 2-2.5-mm pale green three-cut beads

No. 31 (Earrings)

Copper wire: 70cm 22-gauge natural wire, 320cm 28-gauge natural wire

Beads: 2 8-mm round pink designer beads

Findings: Gold ear wires

Instructions for No. 30

1. Use Twist 'n' Curl to make a single coil; wind coil around a glass bead.

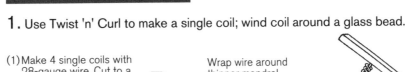

(1) Make 4 single coils with 28-gauge wire. Cut to a length of 8cm (see p. 15).

Wrap wire around thinner mandrel.

8cm

(2) Pass 22-gauge wire through single coil.

(3) Insert mandrel into 8-mm glass bead.

(4) Wrap single coil around glass bead.

Cut here.
22-gauge wire
3mm
3mm
1.5cm

2. Use Twist 'n' Curl to make 3 beaded wire beads (see p. 57).

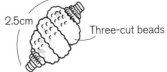

2.5cm
Three-cut beads

3. Make necklace components.

See Step 2 on p. 58 for A, B, and C.
See Step 7 on p. 58 for D and E.

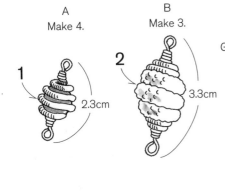

A
Make 4.

1
2.3cm

B
Make 3.

2
3.3cm

C
Make 6.

Green bead
1.5cm

D
3mm
7cm 22-gauge wire
5-mm and 8-mm designer beads
(Make 1 of each.)
8mm

E
5mm
8-mm designer bead
Make 13.
8mm

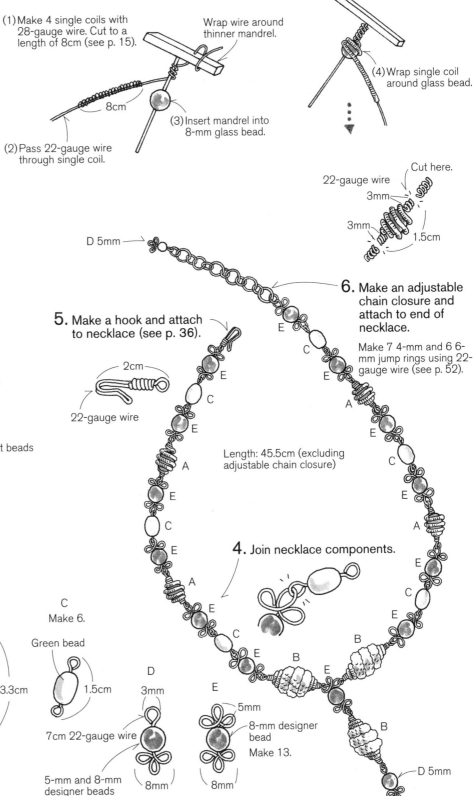

D 5mm

5. Make a hook and attach to necklace (see p. 36).

2cm
22-gauge wire

6. Make an adjustable chain closure and attach to end of necklace.

Make 7 4-mm and 6 6-mm jump rings using 22-gauge wire (see p. 52).

Length: 45.5cm (excluding adjustable chain closure)

4. Join necklace components.

E
C
A
E
C
E
A
E
C
E
A
E
C
E
B
B
B
D 5mm

E
E
A
E
C
E
A
E
C
E

(Instructions for No. 31 are on p. 61.)

No. 32 (p. 19)
Tools and Supplies

Twist 'n' Curl (see p. 15 for instructions)

No. 32 (Choker)

Copper wire: 90cm 22-gauge silver wire, 3m 28-gauge white wire
Beads: 612 1.5-mm silver seed beads, 4-mm fire-polished beads (6 each rose and light amethyst, 9 each olivine, sapphire, smoke gray, and topaz)
Other supplies: 4 silver bead tips, 8 15-mm silver eyepins, silver spring clasp, silver adjustable chain closure, 3m 0.36mm clear nylon-coated wire, 6 silver crimp beads

Instructions for No. 32

1. Use Twist 'n' Curl to make 3 beaded wire beads (see p. 57).

2cm — Silver beads

2. Make choker components.

Eyepin

Fire-polished bead

3mm

Round end with round-nose pliers.

Arrangement of fire-polished beads
A: Topaz
B: Smoke gray
C: Sapphire
D: Olivine
Make 2 of each.

9mm

Cut wire, leaving 9-mm end. → 1cm

5. Attach bead tips (see p. 58).

Clasp
B D
A C
1cm 1cm
2cm 2cm
2cm 2cm

Length: 38cm (excluding adjustable chain closure)

2cm 2cm
3cm

String 1cm silver beads at ends, 2cm elsewhere.

4. String beads on nylon-coated wire.
● Olivine
○ Topaz
○ Silver

4
● Smoke gray
○ Sapphire
○ Silver

6. Make circular components that go between top and bottom strands of choker.

Center of 180cm nylon-coated wire Start here.

2cm

String beads on nylon-coated wire. Attach to top and bottom of choker, as shown above.

● Light amethyst
○ Rose

String crimp beads on nylon-coated wire and compress with pliers. Cut excess wire.

Crimp beads

7. Attach components made in Step 2 and findings to bead tips attached in Step 6.

(Instructions for opening jump rings are on p. 37.)

Clasp

Adjustable chain closure

3. Attach bead tips to 2 60-cm lengths nylon-coated wire (see p. 58).

2cm 2cm
2cm 2cm
1cm 1cm

C B
D A

Adjustable chain closure

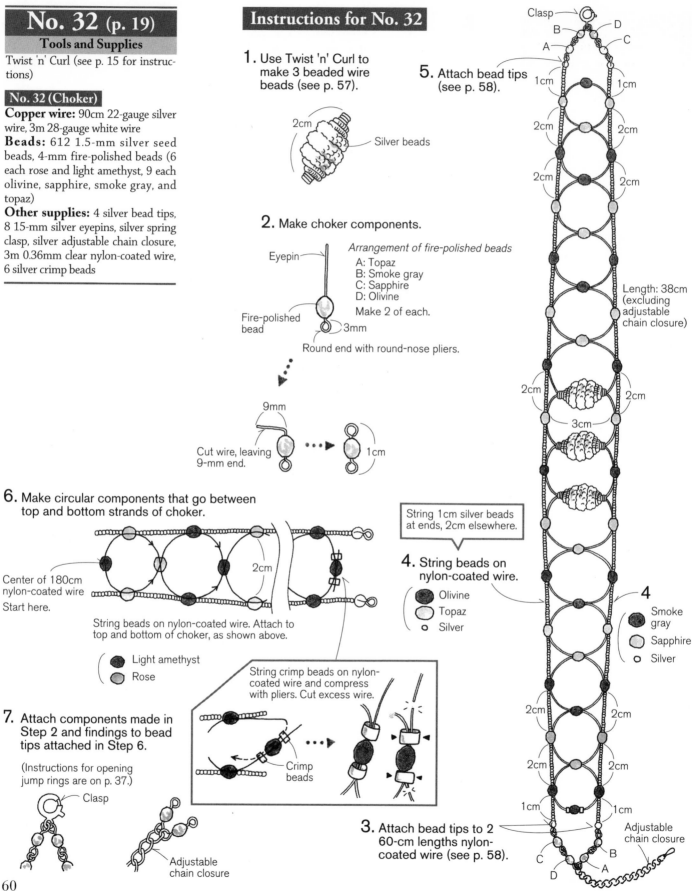

No. 33, 34, 35
(p. 20)

Tools and Supplies

Twist 'n' Curl (see p. 15 for instructions)

No. 33 (Cell phone strap)

Copper wire: 170cm 22-gauge natural wire, 2m 28-gauge natural wire
Beads: 292 2-2.5-mm pale blue three-cut beads, aqua fire-polished beads (12 3-mm, 6 4-mm)
Other supplies: Small strap with ring

No. 34 (Cell phone strap)

Copper wire: 170cm 22-gauge silver wire, 2m 28-gauge lavender wire
Beads: 292 2-2.5-mm purple three-cut beads, amethyst fire-polished beads (12 3-mm, 6 4-mm)
Other supplies: Small strap with ring

No. 35 (Cell phone strap)

Copper wire: 170cm 22-gauge silver wire, 2m 28-gauge white wire
Beads: 292 2-2.5-mm white three-cut beads, fire-polished beads (12 3-mm blue zircon, 6 4-mm white)
Other supplies: Small strap with ring

∗ No. 33, 34 and No. 35 differ in colors used only.

Instructions for No. 33, 34, 35

1. Use Twist 'n' Curl to make 2 beaded wire beads (see p. 57).

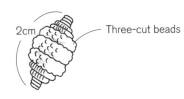

2cm — Three-cut beads

2. Make connectors for beads made in Step 1.

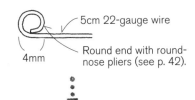

5cm 22-gauge wire
4mm — Round end with round-nose pliers (see p. 42).

Insert wire into bead.

Cut wire, leaving a 1-cm end. Round with round-nose pliers.

3cm

Make 2 beads of the same length.

3. Make 6 each of A, B, and C.

5.5cm 22-gauge wire

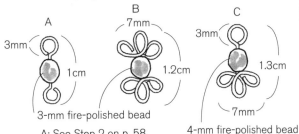

A
3mm
1cm
3-mm fire-polished bead
A: See Step 2 on p. 58.
B: See Step 7 on p. 58.

B
7mm
1.2cm

C
3mm
1.3cm
7mm
4-mm fire-polished bead

6. Attach joined sections to purchased strap.

5. Join sections of strap, alternating between A and B.

Length: 10cm (excluding purchased strap)

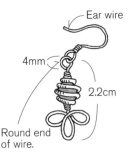

A A
A B A
A B

C C

4. Attach C to beaded wire beads made in Step 2.

Close rings tightly so they won't come apart (instructions for opening jump rings are on p. 37).

Close with pliers.

Instructions for No. 31

1. Use Twist 'n' Curl to make 2 single coils. Wrap coils around designer beads.

1.5cm

(See Step 1 on p. 59.)

2. Make other sections.

10cm 22-gauge wire
See Step 7 on p. 58.
8mm

3. Attach ear wires.

Ear wire
4mm
2.2cm
Round end of wire.

61

No. 36 (p. 21)

Tools and Supplies

WigJig Delphi, Twist 'n' Curl (see p. 10 and 15 for instructions)

No. 36 (Necklace)

Copper wire: 210cm 20-gauge silver wire, 360cm 28-gauge yellow wire

Beads: 13 6-mm blue fire-polished beads, 420 2-2.5-mm yellow three-cut beads

Findings: Silver spring clasp, silver adjustable chain closure, 2 3 x 4-mm silver jump rings

Instructions for No. 36

1. Use WigJig Delphi to make 10 motifs.

Peg placement

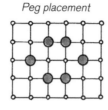

10cm 20-gauge wire

End here. (3) (5)
(6) (1) 1.5cm
(2) (4) Start here.
1.5cm

3. Use Twist 'n' Curl to make 2 beaded wire beads (see p. 50).

String 30cm three-cut beads. 3cm

2. Wrap wire around 4 of the motifs.

60cm 28-gauge wire

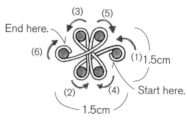

Wind wire tightly.

End here. End here.
End here.

Don't wind wire here.

Length: 42cm (excluding adjustable chain closure)

4. Make wire coils.

(1) Use Twist 'n' Curl to make single coils.

28-gauge wire
11cm
Make 2.
Thinner mandrel

(3) Insert wire into coil.
20cm

(2) Round end of 50cm 20-gauge wire with round-nose pliers.

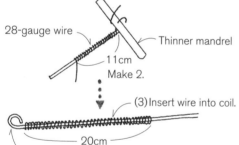
1.8cm 2.5cm

(4) Bend coil into shape with your hands.

5. Pass 20-gauge wire through beads.

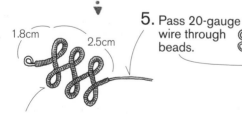

Coil made in Step 4

Fire-polished bead

3 3

9. Attach findings (instructions for opening jump rings are on p. 37).

Clasp
Jump ring

Adjustable chain closure

8. Join sections made in Steps 1, 2, and 7.

6. Make second single coil (see Step 4) and attach to other beaded wire bead.

Round end of wire.

7. Make 12 beaded connectors.

5cm 22-gauge wire

3mm
1.2cm Fire-polished bead

(See Step 2 on p. 58.)

Motif made in Step 2

Motif made in Step 1

Connector made in Step 7

No. 37, 38, 39
(p. 23)
Tools and supplies

Wire Worker (see p. 22 for instructions)

No. 37 (Bracelet)
Copper wire: 180cm 22-gauge natural wire, 410cm 20-gauge silver wire
Beads: 7 8-mm blue fire-polished beads, 336 1.6-mm purple Delica beads (DB-111-C)

No. 38 (Bracelet)
Copper wire: 250cm 22-gauge silver wire
Beads: 2.5-mm triangle beads (41 pale blue, 43 purple), 2 8-mm blue fire-polished beads

No. 39 (Earrings)
Copper wire: 120cm 20-gauge silver wire
Beads: 2 8-mm blue fire-polished beads
Findings: Silver ear wires

Instructions for No. 38

1. Use Wire Worker to make a single coil.

Flat mandrel — Wind 2m wire.

(See p. 15 for instructions.)

1.5cm — Remove from mandrel and stretch to 17cm.

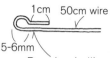

2. Make inner section of bracelet.

1cm 50cm wire

5-6mm

Round end with round-nose pliers.

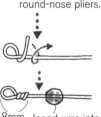

8mm Insert wire into fire-polished bead.

3. Insert inner section into single coil made in Step 1.

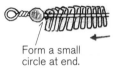

Form a small circle at end.

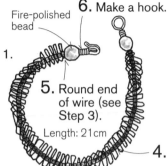

Fire-polished bead

6. Make a hook.

5. Round end of wire (see Step 3).

Length: 21cm

4. String triangle beads at random on inner section.

How to make a hook

Bend wire.

3cm
1.5cm 3cm

Wrap wire and cut excess.

1.5cm
6mm

3. Complete 6 sections begun in Steps 1 and 2.

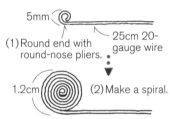

5mm

(1) Round end with round-nose pliers.

25cm 20-gauge wire

1.2cm (2) Make a spiral.

(Side view)

(3) Bend wire at a right angle.

(4) Insert wire into beaded coil.

(6) Make another spiral.

(5) Insert wire into square coil made in Step 2.

2.5cm

Repeat Step 3, forming a right angle.

Instructions for No. 37

1. Use Wire Worker to make 6 beaded single coils (see Steps 2 - 4 on p. 15).

2cm

String 8cm beads on 22-gauge wire. Use thin, round mandrel.

2. Again with Wire Worker, make a single coil.

Using the square mandrel, wind 2m 20-gauge wire.

Remove from mandrel and stretch to 12cm.

2cm

Cut into 6 2-cm lengths.

4. Make inner section of bracelet.

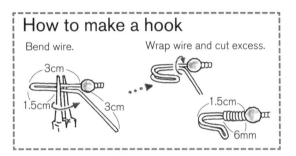

Round end of wire, following Step 2 of instructions for No. 38.

60cm 20-gauge wire

Length: 25cm

Fire-polished bead

3

6. Make a hook.

5. String fire-polished beads and components made in Step in alternation.

Instructions for No. 39

4. Insert wire into bead. Round end of component made in Step 1 (see Step 3 of No. 38).

3. Insert inner section made in Step 1 into coil.

1. Use the Wire Worker's square mandrel to make a single coil with 64cm 20-gauge wire.

2. Make inner sections.
Follow directions in (1)-(3) of Step 3 of No.37. Make 2.

1.5cm

Cut into 2 1.5-cm sections. Make 2.

6. Attach ear wires.

3.5cm

5. Round end of inner section (see Step 2 of No. 38).

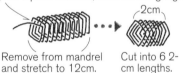

No. 40, 41, 42, 43
(p. 24)
Tools and Supplies

Wire Worker (see p. 22 for instructions)

No. 40 (Bracelet)
Copper wire: 30cm 20-gauge silver wire, 6m 22-gauge silver wire
Beads: 3 8-mm round purple plastic beads, 300 2.5-mm blue triangle beads

No. 41 (Bracelet)
Copper wire: 30cm 20-gauge copper wire, 6m 22-gauge copper wire
Beads: 3 8-mm round green plastic beads, 300 2.5-mm gold triangle beads

No. 42 (Necklace)
Copper wire: 45cm 20-gauge silver wire, 530cm 22-gauge silver wire
Beads: 7 8-mm round purple plastic beads, 2 6 x 7-mm antique silver plastic bicone beads, 200 2.5-mm blue triangle beads
Other supplies: 90cm 1.5-mm natural leather cord

No. 43 (Necklace)
Copper wire: 45cm 20-gauge copper wire, 530cm 22-gauge copper wire
Beads: 7 8-mm round green plastic beads, 2 6 x 7-mm antique gold plastic bicone beads, 200 2.5- mm gold triangle beads
Other supplies: 90cm 1.5-mm natural leather cord

∗ No. 40 and No. 41, and No. 42 and No. 43 differ in colors used only.

Instructions for No. 42, 43

1. Use Wire Worker to make 2 beaded single coils (see Steps 2 - 4 on p. 15).
Wind 20cm beads strung on 22-gauge wire.

5cm
1cm
1cm   Use thin, round mandrel.

3. Use Wire Worker to make a single coil.
Thin, round mandrel
3cm
1.5cm   1.5cm   22-gauge wire
Cut into 1.5-cm lengths.

4. Make inner section.
45cm 20-gauge wire
5-6mm   Follow Step 2 in instructions for No. 38 on p. 63.

6. Pass wire through section made in Step 3, then section made in Step 2.

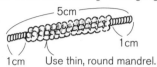

3
2

2. Use Wire Worker to make a single coil.
Wind 22-gauge wire, using triangular mandrel.
9cm
3cm
(1) Wind so that wire doesn't stretch.
(2) Cut into 3-cm lengths.
(3) Insert a plastic bead into the center of each 3-cm length.
No. 42: Purple
No. 43: Green
1.5cm   1.5cm
(3 coils)

11. Tie leather cord.
45cm
Secure with glue.

10. Round end of inner wire (see Step 4).

12. Add beads and tie ends of cord.

5. String bicone bead on inner wire.
No. 42: Antique silver
No. 43: Antique gold

8. Pass wire through section made in Step 3.

9. Add other bicone bead.

1   2   1

7. Pass wire through section made in Step 1, then section made in Step 2.
Length: 40cm (excluding leather cord)

Instructions for No. 40, 41

1. }
2. } Make 3 sections of bracelet, following instructions for No. 42 and No. 43.

3. Make inner section.
30cm 20-gauge wire
(1) Follow instructions in Step 2 of No. 38 on p. 63.
4-5mm
(2) Pass wire through sections made in Steps 1 and 2 in alternation.

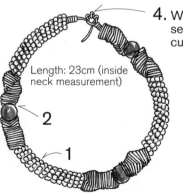

Length: 23cm (inside neck measurement)
2
1

4. Wind end of wire extending from inner section around ring at end of bracelet; cut excess wire.

Hide end of wire on coil made in Step 2.

Hide end of wire inside coil.

64